ANOTHER COUNTRY, ANOTHER KING

Richard Holloway was born in Glasgow in 1933, and began his theological studies at Kelham in 1948, with a break for national service in the army, 1952–53. After leaving Kelham in 1956 he served as secretary to the Bishop of Accra (1956–58), and then completed his studies in Edinburgh, London and New York. He was ordained deacon in 1959 and priest in June 1960. He has served parishes in Glasgow, Edinburgh, Boston (USA) and Oxford, and became Bishop of Edinburgh in 1986.

D1646185

RICHARD HOLLOWAY

ANOTHER COUNTRY, ANOTHER KING

FOUNT

An Imprint of
HarperCollins *Publishers*

William Collins Sons & Co. Ltd
London . Glasgow . Sydney . Auckland
Toronto . Johannesburg

First published in Great Britain in 1991 by Fount Paperbacks

Fount Paperbacks is an imprint of
Collins Religious Division,
part of the HarperCollins Publishing Group
77–85 Fulham Palace Road, London W6 8JB

Typeset by Medcalf Type Ltd, Bicester, Oxon
Printed and bound in Great Britain by
Cox & Wyman Ltd, Reading

In memory of Roger Allan Moore

CONTENTS

PREFACE

Although it is a slightly misleading way to put it, this is a book about the Christian creed. The word creed comes, of course, from the Latin verb *believe*. The creed is a summary of what Christians believe. But there is a catch. Many people go to church and say the creed when it comes in the service, but they are uneasy about it. Bits of it they can recite with integrity, bits of it they are uncertain about, and some bits they just cannot accept. Even so, they want to be in church, however uncomfortably, and they want to identify themselves with Christianity. Is this dishonest or hypocritical, they want to know? Is it right to go to church only if you subscribe enthusiastically to the creed, the official summary of the Christian faith?

We all know, of course, that there are many people who attend church and say the creed who do not strictly "believe" it. Some of them are people on the way in, some of them are on the way out. Some are searchers who are coming to faith, however hesitantly; some are withdrawers, people who are losing their faith, or from whom the faith is being withdrawn. Philip Larkin the poet was asked at the end of his life why he did not write poetry any more. He replied that it was not he who had left poetry, but poetry that had left him. That is the experience many people have with faith. It leaves them. They find themselves, often against their own desire, without it. For some of these, often nostalgic ex-believers, the problem is a kind of intellectual scrupulosity.

They think the creed has to be believed in a particular way, what some would describe as "literally" or "fundamentally", and they know, for instance, that they can no longer accord Hell a literal existence. A metaphor, perhaps, a way of describing an intense evil, a conviction that wickedness should be punished and righteousness vindicated – all of these are uses they can find for the word Hell, but they are no longer able to believe in it as a place of everlasting torment. As a matter of fact, I try to address this very subject in Chapter 7 of this book, but I raise it here because it presents us with a particularly vivid example of the kind of difficulty some people run into with Christian faith. If you no longer find yourself able to subscribe "literally" to every clause in the Christian creed does that mean you should abandon it? Well, that may be the honest thing for some people to do, but it does not necessarily follow for all. The creed is what *Christians* believe, though it does not necessarily follow that every single Christian will recite it or understand it in the same way. Some will recite it enthusiastically, some with increasing discomfort and some tentatively, exploringly. I believe there is room for all these responses, because the creed ought not to be seen as a legal statement with hard edges. It is a summary of the ways in which Christians have tried to describe their experience of God, Jesus Christ and the Church. And the experience is always what counts. There was a time, after all, when there was no creed, but there were Christian believers.

This book is an attempt to get behind the creed, the summary of faith, to the experience of faith. Over the years I have conducted what are called "missions" in various places. In this sense a mission is an organized event which has at its centre a systematic exposition of the Christian faith.

Such an exposition is not an argument aimed at persuading people, by a kind of intellectual force, to accept the Christian position. At any rate, that is not what I have been led to do over the years. There is a mystery about the birth of faith. Christians believe it is a gift from God. That is why people should not be manipulated or scared into it, for that is to usurp the work of God. Nevertheless, part of the mystery of faith is that we know people often receive it when the Gospel is preached to them, the Christian message is explained or shared. I shall attempt to explain something of the mystery of coming to faith in Chapter 6. In this book I set out to share my faith, to describe how I hold to the Christian creed. The chapters are not systematic expositions of clauses in the creed, but they do attempt to wrestle with the mysteries of faith that the creed summarizes: God, Christ, the Holy Spirit, the Forgiveness of Sins, the Church and Sacraments, Judgement and the Return of Christ. I have tried to be as inclusive as possible, because I believe that the community of faith is larger than certain spiritual monopolists would claim and there is room in it for most people.

This book began its formation as I prepared the Mission to Oxford University, which I led in the Lent Term 1989. The Mission was an experience I shall never forget and I would like to salute all those who took part. The book is dedicated to my friend Roger Moore, Senior Warden at the Church of the Advent in Boston, Massachusetts, who died before it was published. If I had wanted a multiple dedication, however, it would have included Roderick Strange, who was Catholic Chaplain at Oxford during the Mission, Brian Mountford, Vicar of the University Church, and all the Assistant Missioners, but especially Paolo and

Jang from the Community at Taizé, who contributed so much to the Mission.

And I owe a special debt of gratitude to my secretary, Christine Roy, for all her patient labours in preparing the book for the publisher.

Richard Holloway
Edinburgh
August 1990

PART I

1

ANOTHER COUNTRY

People who speak thus make it clear that
they are seeking a homeland. (Hebrews
11:14)

There is a Monty Python sketch of four businessmen from
the North of England sitting in their pin-striped suits, after
a heavy night out, comparing notes on how deprived their
childhood was. One of them begins by saying, "When a were
a lad, we lived in cardboard box at top of slagheap and every
morning slag from local pit would come up rail and be poured
on top of us and we'd be burned to death." The man next
to him would reply, "Luxury! Sheer luxury! When a were a
lad, we lived in paper bag at bottom of cesspit and every
morning . . ." – but we need not go on to describe how each
capped the other's story with a more preposterous tale of early
deprivation. I found myself in a rather Pythonesque situation
some time ago. I was having lunch with a friend whom I had
always thought of as a quintessential member of the English
establishment. He had gone to Winchester and Oxford and
was then head of a department in a famous national
institution. I was in a confessional kind of mood and told him
that I had always felt myself to be an "outsider" and had never
really felt totally at home in any of the institutions I'd lived
or worked in. I didn't exactly go in for a Pythonesque
description of my childhood as being the source of this feeling,

15

but I suggested, I suppose, that it had something to do with it. He didn't actually reply, "Luxury! Sheer luxury!", and go on to describe his own particular pattern of early deprivation, but he did point out that if you really wanted to know what being an "outsider" was, then go to Winchester, and go to Oxford, and feel yourself to be a boy looking in on these great institutions but never really at home in them. His reply disappointed me, because I was beginning to develop a proprietorial attitude to "outsidership" and I was reluctant to share it with someone who seemed to me to be manifestly on the *inside* of things.

But something else happened later that confirmed a growing sense I had that there weren't as many insiders around as I thought. I was lecturing to a quintessentially insider group – what the pay code of the Church Commissioners of the Church of England describes as "dignitaries": bishops, deans, archdeacons and people like that. Again, I adopted a somewhat confessional tone in what I chose to say to them. I talked about the dilemma of the private person in the public place, what W. H. Auden called "private faces in public places". I often feel that the true status of the Christian disciple is to be in a permanent state of aspiration and longing after something which he or she does not yet possess. In fact, all Christians are in that position but the profession of Christian leadership seems to contradict it. It seems to imply the status of possession not aspiration, of arrival not pilgrimage. All doubt and uncertainty banished, Christian leaders are official public believers. All moral struggle at an end, their weaknesses vanquished, they are the inviolate upholders of the perfect standard. Well, it isn't really like that and most of us who are these public faces with private faces behind them often feel like frauds, pulled between our own inner uncertainties and the expectations of the public. But it's even more profound than that; it's more than being unable to fulfil the unreal expectations people have of us. There is a sense in which fraudulence is intrinsic to our role, is almost part of our vocation. Paul has a mysterious sentence in his second letter to the Corinthians that captures it: "We are the imposters who have to speak the truth, the unknown men whom all men know" (2 Corinthians 6:8).

In my talk to this group of dignitaries, I admitted to a tension between my private personality and my public role. I talked about this private person and its own limitations, doubts and struggles, tagged on to this figure who swans around in theatrical costume talking, talking, always talking. As a public man I am a professional Christian, but as a private man I am very much an amateur Christian, an ordinary aspiring learner. I wasn't sure if the assembled dignitaries would feel the same tension (after all, a Church of England bishop is a sort of archetypical insider), but I discovered in my discussions that almost all of them felt the way I did. They felt this gap between their public roles and their private struggles; they, too, were private faces in public places: the danger being, of course, that the public face can take over totally and swamp the private person, so that there no longer *is* a private person but only a sort of pompous, public figure always pronouncing and apparently confident, never owning to failure or feebleness.

I don't want to draw any elaborate conclusions from these two experiences, but I am increasingly aware that behind the confident exteriors that most people wear like masks, there is often a very different reality. Many people, if not most people, are just a little bit baffled by life. They feel thrown into it, almost as though they'd been shoved on to

17

a stage to take part in a play whose lines they hadn't learned, and whose script they had never seen; yet the curtain is up and there is an audience out there and they are expected somehow to fit into the drama that is unrolling.

Ours is a rather confessional era and while it has its dangers it has some strengths. One of the things that we have discovered in our time is the value of shared vulnerability. There are many groups whose therapeutic role is based on this recognition. People who are addicted to damaging behaviour of one sort or another – alcohol abuse, drug abuse, sexual abuse, over-eating and so on – find not only solace but strength and understanding in sharing their vulnerabilities, in owning to others the gap between the exterior confident person and the inner person who is lacking in confidence, is frail, maybe even terrified. There might have been societies where this conflict was not known, this sense of being something of an outsider in a world filled, apparently, with insiders. There might have been societies filled with self-confident people who knew exactly who they were and where they were going. But that, anyway, is not the kind of society we inhabit. We live to a very great extent nowadays in an individualistic and atomized society, in which there are few binding social myths or commonly received truths that mediate meaning to us and give us our private and our public roles. Ours is a free-market universe, which can be as baffling to the outsider as a visit to the stock exchange, with its incessant din and insiders' language and signal system.

And religious communities can be just as baffling as that to the outsider. They can suggest to the searcher or doubter an absolutely closed and insulated world peopled by individuals who use a mysterious sort of "inspeak" and occupy an impenetrable fastness of mysterious certainty.

Well, that kind of situation does exist, but many of the people who are on the inside of religious communities are much closer to the outside than they appear to be; and many people on the outside look with wistfulness at these apparently closed circles of faith and yet feel themselves compelled by honest doubt to remain for ever outside. Some who are *in* always seem close to being out, and some who are *out* always seem close to being in. But it may be that we have misunderstood the situation and are using the wrong kind of images, as though spiritual states were like gentlemen's clubs or social élites. Certainly, Jesus seemed to repudiate this understanding of religion. "Not every one who calls me Lord, Lord, will enter the kingdom of heaven," he said to a group of apparent insiders (Matthew 7:21); and, "Enter my kingdom, for inasmuch as you did it to one of the least of these my brethren, you did it to me," he said to a group of apparent outsiders (Matthew 25:34, 40). Apparently, things aren't always what they seem to be, so maybe we ought to abandon some of our presuppositions and think again about the meaning of things.

The main difficulty for human beings, of course, is that they *do think*: they muse about their own experiences, about life and its inevitable end in death, and their own place in the scheme of things. As far as we can tell, other parts of the animate creation do not seem to have this type of self-consciousness. Animals seem to be capable of feeling as well as inflicting pain, but they seem to behave in a programmed, instinctive or automatic way, largely or mainly to do with breeding and feeding and fighting for survival. Human beings do all those things as well, but they also have this strange ability to observe themselves and ask questions about the meaning of life itself.

Irresistibly, I am drawn back to the insider/outsider motif. As I have already said, we are thrown unprepared into life, and bewilderment results. I detect several forms of this bewilderment, or, to be more honest, have experienced several forms of it. The first is almost physical. Where did it all come from? Has it any meaning, any beginning, end or purpose? In our time our knowledge of the size and age of the universe has expanded in a bewildering if not terrifying way. 'The eternal silence of these infinite spaces terrifies me', said Blaise Pascal and contemplating the vastness of the universe can reduce us to a sense of insignificant absurdity. We are only a reed shaken in the wind. Our anguish comes from the fact that, to quote Pascal again, though we are only a reed, we are a *thinking* reed, and it is thought that brings bewilderment. Contemplating the physical universe and our own tiny niche in it can lead to a sense of fatalism or brute acceptance. The thing is simply there, simply given, seems to have no beginning and no end, and has only the meaning we impose upon it. One scientific genius[1] tells us that the universe is like a ball, self-contained, apparently self-generating, possibly self-destructing; and like a ball it has no beginning and no end to it, it simply *is*. And my life and your life are little flecks of foam, thrown up for a moment, by the great onrush of meaningless time – we were born, we shall die, and that's that.

There's nothing, nothing, nothing, not a breath beyond . . .
The heart is not a clock, it will not wind again,
The dead are but dead, there is no use for them,
They neither care, nor care not, they are only dead.

wrote Sacheverell Sitwell.[2]

Finding personal meaning in such a universe is difficult. Close up, life can be confusing and difficult to handle, but from a great way off a kind of pattern can be discerned. It's a bit like gazing out on a piece of meadow or woodland on a brilliant summer afternoon. Beneath the composed and apparently idyllic scene there is a desperate quest for survival going on, in which birds are hunting insects, larger birds are hunting rodents, cattle are being fattened for the local abattoir, and the very trees and flowers are living and dying, shedding their leaves endlessly in the grand and determinate cycle of nature. Seen from afar there is a kind of pattern to it (a great food chain, in fact, seems to be the best description of it), in which one species preys upon another. From a distance the overall spectacle even has a kind of terrible beauty to it. Seen close up, however, it can be appalling, as a fly struggles vainly in the spider's web, or a rabbit shrieks against the trap, or a trout struggles against the talons of the osprey which has just snatched it from the river. It is possible to stand a great way off and look at the human scene with a similar detachment. Seen from this scientific distance we are a part of that same self-devouring chain of supply and demand, of life, survival and death. Up close it can be tragic, but from a serene distance it's just the way things are. From that distance we don't see the faces of the people at the bedside of the dying child, or the terror in the eyes of the captive before his torturers. We only see the process through which the great universe remorselessly devours its children and propagates more. The anguish we feel is entirely the result of this strange chance of nature that has given us consciousness, made us *thinking* reeds instead of mere reeds that are cut down and die without awareness, pain or enjoyment.

Knowing how to live and be true to ourselves, in the midst of this great and apparently meaningless chain of being, is difficult. We can, of course, choose to impose local meaning upon events. We can be true to our friends; we can give ourselves to the pursuit of happiness, however we perceive it; we can find some work to do that interests us. These are all little acts of private defiance against the great surrounding absurdity; little impositions of meaning, like cave drawings by dwellers underground.

One way to deal with the experience of bewilderment as we search for meaning in and to our lives, therefore, is this way of private survival, with purely private loyalties. And this way of looking at reality and our inconsequential part in it has its own honesty and courage. It is sometimes called *objective consciousness*, because it is based on a cool appraisal of harsh, actual, empirical reality and not upon any romantic wishful thinking. And it does put us in touch with half of reality, the bit that's on the outside, the country that's before our eyes and is available to the camera in our surveillance machine as we fly over the terrain and take accurate photographs of it. There we see it all, the hills and the valleys, the rivers, the great plains, the villages, the cities; only if we get too near do we hear the noises – the laughter, the screams, the grinding of the great chain as it moves inexorably along its groove.

But this kind of consciousness does not seem able to provide a picture or give us an account of another type of reality that our cameras and techniques are less able to probe. There seems to be a sort of *inner* reality, a dimension of inner space that human beings inhabit just as self-consciously as they inhabit the physical universe. There is a consciousness that gazes in upon itself gazing out, or watches itself watching, knows itself knowing, hears itself hearing, and so on to the point of bewilderment. And this other, inner, consciousness seems to catch glimpses or hear rumours of another country, another universe, another reality, that seems mysteriously interfused with this measurable universe, but is not simply, or seems to be more than simply, an aspect of it. Most people at some time, some exceptional people most of the time, seem to be strongly aware of and drawn towards that other country, the invisible reality that seems to pervade the solidity of the universe. Of course, the really committed exponents of objective consciousness are able to fit this mysterious longing into their account of reality. To them it's a sort of distraction, a kind of wishful thinking, or projection on to external reality of our desire not to die; we possess a myth-making facility, a powerful ability to weave creative and consoling fantasies that protect us against the harshness of the actual universe. It is not easy to repudiate this account of these longings and intimations, because they do not command the kind of hard evidence that seems to be available as support for the great theory of the autonomous universe. Many of the cleverest people alive today would deal thus with the whole spiritual hypothesis, and see it simply as an inconsequential daydream, an hallucinatory aside, entirely explicable from within a self-creating, self-explaining, self-existent and self-destructive universe.

Convincing as this account of these longings is, on one level, it does not seem ultimately persuasive to many intelligent and often rather wise human beings. There is no way of avoiding some kind of circularity in argument here, whatever way we choose to go, but the manner in which objective consciousness dismisses the sense of another presence in the universe seems particularly question-begging. It says that it is the universe itself which creates this intimation of a reality that transcends the universe. The physical universe generates dreams, longings and intimations of another reality, another country that exists only in the human imagination.

This explanation may be consistent, but it still begs the question. For if there *is* another reality which influences our nature, no amount of analysis of our nature alone will either put us in touch with the alleged other reality or prove to us that it does not exist. It is not enough to look at a man looking at something, in order to account for his behaviour. We have to try looking at what he's looking *at*, in order to know what he's doing. I daresay it would be possible by ignoring the moon to develop a satisfactory explanation for the existence of tides without reference to any external influence: and people have certainly found explanations for the religious impulse that are consistent with their conception of the closed universe. But none of that can absolutely demonstrate the absence of another cause for these impulses and longings, namely a transcendent reality that exerts an influence on us, both positive and negative, drawing some men and women towards itself with irresistible certainty, and invading others with a mysterious sense of sadness and loss, because they cannot find their way towards the other country they seem to have been born remembering.

There are good reasons for committing ourselves to either hypothesis. For many intelligent people the whole business comes down to an assessment of probabilities and a commitment to the more likely hypothesis. I have never found that particular approach congenial, however, though I do not deny its efficacy for people who are cooler and more rational than I. I have always responded to these inner voices and hungers on a different level, and it seems to me that this other level is insufficiently regarded by those who tend to operate on the basis of pure intelligence. I find myself looking into the distance, mysteriously trying to see the invisible, listening to silence, responding to an imperative that seems to contradict the values of the world. In fact, I find myself in a strange kind of divided state in which I live in two countries and feel the tension between different allegiances. I find myself in a bewildered state, going my way like everyone else, finding some enjoyment "before the night cometh"; but at the same time, I feel myself to be a citizen of another country, hearing the commands and pleadings of another king. And something inside me answers to that other country and its voices with a sort of recognition and a sense of its truthfulness and claim upon me.

That other country and its ruler do not compete well in the noisy market-place of contemporary ideas and values. The sense of its existence comes as a sort of underthought, something heard between words or at the end of the music; and it seems to call forth a response and an attitude that is so at variance with the attitude of the world and the response the world demands, that it is not surprising that it usually goes unheard and unheeded. But what if it is there? What if it is true and real? It cannot be a matter of indifference, a question as great as that. If there *is* another country which we somehow inhabit, another king towards whom some strange allegiance is due, then it surely cannot be a matter that does not concern our own happiness. It would be something that affected us totally. It may be that our indifference to it, or our failure to find it, is the cause of some of our confusions and moral dislocations, our sense of powerlessness in the face of all the complicated evils and sorrows of history, our sense that so many of the things that are, ought not to be. If there is no other country, no other king, then these are vain and tragic longings and we are cursed with compassion in an unfeeling universe, cursed with the longing for value and purpose in a universe that is simply a brute fact without value or meaning, except the temporary value we impose upon it. But if there is another country, another king, then it would account for much; it would account for the mysterious longings that we often discover in ourselves to give ourselves to some great thing; it would account for the courage that some of the most attractive people in history have shown, the courage to give up life itself for a cause beyond life. It would be a sufficient explanation for the extraordinary existence of great holiness in a few flaming souls in every generation. The reality of the other country would account for those strange places "which also are the world's end", in Eliot's phrase,[3] places that call out to something in us, call us towards the holy, towards some great and nameless good, not known, yet haunting our imagination.

But the issue cannot be decided in an armchair. The Christian faith calls itself a way, a journey, a pilgrimage; in an old phrase, it calls us to a life of "experimental divinity"; it calls us to trust the voice we hear from a long way off and to look towards the light invisible and struggle towards it.

Thomas Carlyle described the two attitudes we have been discussing as the two grand Antagonisms. We could describe them as Reason and Revelation, though it would be wrong to suggest that they are in necessary opposition, although they often do find themselves opposed.

By Reason I mean that urge in human nature to account for the way things are. Reason tends to be active, assertive, investigative, cool, controlling, restless; probing, rather than receptive. If it were fashionable to say these things nowadays, we might describe it as a pre-eminently masculine characteristic and we would find that one of the best ways to capture its style and effect, as well as its limitations, would be to use male sexual imagery. It is no accident, I think, that when we think of all conquering Rationality working without sufficient sensitivity to other, more subtle realities, we talk about raping the environment, or violating the earth, or riding rough-shod over the weak.

By Revelation on the other hand, I mean something more fragile and less assertive. Those who would receive Revelation need to be open to it, need to wait upon it. They need to be empty, not absolutely sure of themselves, because only empty cups can be filled. Again, sexual imagery suggests itself and the models are all feminine, or what it was once fashionable to characterize as feminine: passive rather than active, receptive rather than assertive, open to being discovered rather than probing and searching, expectant rather than defensive. Maggie Ross[4] says that God cannot be posited; God can only be engaged or encountered. We can posit something and *call it* God, but it is the work of our own minds, and while our minds are drawn to understand and seek knowledge of the mystery of God, the primary experience is encounter with a Revealed Mystery. William Temple said that two things were needed for effective Revelation: a divinely controlled event and minds attuned to receive it right. But minds, like radio receivers, can be defective and pick up nothing.

The balance between Reason and sensitivity to Revelation

varies from person to person and from religion to religion. Some stress Revelation, the great given thing from Outside to which we must submit without argument; others stress Reason, because it is part of our nature to ask questions and not just to take orders. Each emphasis has its dangers: there are religions that are so demanding and irrational that they offend against our nature, producing a type of person who is hard and fanatical, claiming to know everything about that invisible mystery we call God. And the other emphasis can produce people who are so dry and rational and sceptical that they are not open even to the possibility of mystery and spirit; they cut themselves off from whole continents of experience and wonder. Some fall for an arrogant over-belief; others fall for an equally arrogant non-belief. Some become spiritually obese and gulp down great quantities of superstition, while others become spiritually anorexic and starve themselves of necessary spiritual truth. Neither seems really complete without the other, which is why Thomas Carlyle described Samuel Johnson and David Hume as the two great half-men of their time:

> It is worthy of note that, in our little British Isle, the two grand Antagonisms of Europe should have stood embodied, under their very highest concentration, in two men produced simultaneously among ourselves. Samuel Johnson and David Hume . . . were children nearly of the same year; through life they were spectators of the same Life-movement; often inhabitants of the same city. Greater contrast, in all things, between two great men, could not be . . .
>
> They were the two half-men of their time: whoso should combine the intrepid Candour and decisive scientific

Clearness of Hume, with the Reverence, the Love and devout Humility of Johnson were the whole man of a new time. Till such whole man arrive for us, and the distracted time admit of such, might the Heavens but bless poor England with half-men worthy to tie the shoe-latchets of these, resembling these even from afar![5]

We might say that these two types of mind and intelligence correspond to the two fundamentally different accounts given about the meaning of the universe: there is the rugged matter-of-*fact*ness on the one hand, that confines itself to the examinable universe and distrusts the reality of anything that cannot be demonstrated or verified in a realistic way; and on the other we have the Johnsonian consciousness, which responds with faith to those strange voices within that talk of a reality beyond this reality. One attitude is sceptical and doubting, to the point of destruction; the other is reverent and filled with wonder and, in Cardinal Newman's phrase, is "on the look out for revelation".

Revelation is the word we always come back to when we think about religion. The premise of the religious claim is that there is another reality beyond this one that yet interfuses with it and makes demands upon it; and since it is obviously unavailable in a straightforward way to the senses that put us in touch with the examinable reality of the universe, if it is real, and not an illusion or an hallucination, it must be revealing itself to us by hints and symbols, experiences and dreams, the whole vocabulary of religious encounter that has been fought over and wrestled with for centuries. Yet the central question remains unanswered and unanswerable in a theoretically final way. Answers seem to range along a continuum that stretches from the absolutely settled conviction that there is no reality behind this language of faith other than the state of mind of those who use it, to those at the other end who have an equally settled conviction that this world of apparently firm reality is like vapour compared to the glory that has been revealed to them, the glory that surrounds that transcendent and supernatural reality called God, the vision of whom reduces the clamours and appetites and very firmness of this world to mist. Between these two apparently impregnable positions human nature in its doubts, struggles and certainties, stretches itself. The difficulty is always in assessing why people locate themselves here rather than there, in this position rather than that, and whether they can be proved right or wrong in doing so. It is always possible, of course, to do the right thing for the wrong reason, to adopt possible positions on erroneous grounds, and much of that goes on in this debate. There is always a great deal of neurotic, not to say pathological religion, but it is equally obvious that there is a great deal of neurotic and pathological unbelief.

Engaging in that kind of superior dredging of the motives of others does not really help. People tend to find themselves helpless before the facts of their own experience. It would be good if there were a genuine ecumenism among truth-searchers, in which they would simply state where they stood and gave a reason for the faith, or the lack of it, they possessed. That, at any rate, is the voice, the tone, the approach, I wish to use in this book. It is true that towering convictions about the wrongness of others can have a magnetic effect, but there is no harm in assuming that most people are honestly seeking truth and meaning in their lives and that they will, at least on one level, want to hear the case that is made by those who believe in the reality of that other country and seek to be obedient to that other king. There are glimpses in the Bible of a gentle and pleading God, who lays before us his quiet claim without shouting at us, and draws us silently with cords of love and compassion rather than using the bullying techniques of the propagandist.

There is a mysterious chant they sing at Taizé –

> We will go by night to seek the source of life,
> thirst alone will be our light.

It comes from the Spanish mystic, St John of the Cross. There is something almost Zen-like in its obscurity and appeal. It speaks to a certain kind of consciousness, and even the strange mixed metaphor of thirst as a lantern or light, somehow twists in the imagination. It is the very existence of the thirst for the source of life, a longing for the end time, which captures and obsesses us, haunts and tantalizes us, so that we are prodded on to the search; or rendered unconsolable, because we know the search can only be a search among our own regrets, since there is no source to which we can go either by day or by night. For me, that search by night is always through the great but tangled traditions of Christian spirituality, for it is inevitable that the glory revealed, the beseechings of God that reach human nature, are muddled and darkened by the way we have understood them.

There are various forms of revelation that we have to reckon with, if we are to discover something of the reality of that other country. But we will not expect to find it perfectly laid forth for us, or perfectly expressed in the lives of other strugglers by night or the institutions they create. However, there is one life that seems to capture the glory that haunts us. The life and words of Jesus Christ can be experienced today in a way that makes his influence contemporary. That statement may baffle the outsider, but the fact is that Jesus Christ always eludes the official burial parties who confidently try to dispose of him. He still encounters people, and he still hangs around the Christian Church, in spite of its ambivalent attitude towards him. The only way to come to any religion is with humility and some scepticism: humility towards the mystery we seek and some scepticism towards the institutions that witness to that mystery. The historian Herbert Butterfield sums this up beautifully: "Cleave to Jesus, and for the rest be uncommitted."

It is possible, of course, to try to turn to Jesus without reference to the Church or Christian community. He himself seemed to exemplify something of the paradox we are describing in his attitude towards religious institutions. He affirmed their necessity and challenged their corruption, so it is unlikely that most of us will be able to do without them. When I am at my lowest point of tolerance for institutional religion, and especially the form of it to which I belong, there are one or two places that bring me back to a sort of good-humoured resignation. There are one or two buildings that heal me, one or two holy places where something of the essence of the glory is distilled and experienced. There are people, some of them dead, who also have that effect: people to whom I can turn – turn again to their combination of mercy and astringency, laughter and heartbreak, and catch sight again of the glory that's revealed; and they are usually people who have operated, however uneasily, within some branch of the Christian Church. That is why I am not too worried if some of our churches are empty, so long as they are open, because some of our churches do their own thing best when they are left alone with God.

And I try to keep my eyes fixed on Jesus, the divine stranger, who always seems to emerge out of the mist. I can't always see him clearly, but I know he stands on the frontier of that other country in a sort of luminous shadow and I travel towards him. The journey is called faith. I have already called it an exercise in experimental divinity, for we are never given the conclusion in advance, only enough light to work by. The length of the experiment is a life and its proof is given to us only in death. We have to say "yes" for a whole lifetime – anything else destroys the experiment. But the experiment of faith is not without its assurances and the greatest of these is holiness. We can never detect this in ourselves and it is spiritually fatal to try, but it comes as a gift to us from others and it is probably the greatest thing we can witness in history. Holiness is a kind of otherness. The holy are totally present to us, that is one of their characteristics, but they are wholly present to something else as well, maybe to something we cannot see. They "endure as seeing him who is invisible". Being in the presence of holiness promotes both sorrow and longing in us and it can even promote hatred. Longing, because it answers to our own heart's desire; sorrow, because we know it costs not less than everything; and hatred because there is in all of us a kind of anger against the light. The holy do not come in stock forms, have no standard vocabulary and usually do not say much about themselves; but they convey a sense of depth, a sense of a hinterland, a sense of belonging also to another country and listening also to another king. We will recognize them because they make almost everyone else seem incomplete. That is one reason why Christians call Jesus *Perfect Man*. Facing him we see holiness, pure otherness. That is what we mean when we say that Jesus Christ is the revelation of God. And by that we do not mean that we have a previous picture of God that we go round trying to fit on to others, the way Prince Charming went round the country with Cinderella's slipper. No, we mean something much more mysterious than that: we mean that we did not know what God was like till we saw this face and believed. There can be no external attestation to such a claim, no authoritative photograph, no genetic fingerprint. Flesh and blood cannot reveal it to us, nor can flesh and blood negate it. But to those of us looking for another country and searching for another king, he comes as he came of old.

2

ANOTHER KING

For while gentle silence enveloped all
things, and night in its swift course was
now half gone, thy all-powerful word
leaped from heaven, from the royal
throne. (Wisdom 18:14–15)

In an article in the *Independent*, Peter Jenkins wrote:

Meyerhold, the great Russian theatre director, used to tell
a story from his days as a law student at Moscow
University. One of the professors would arrange for a
powerful thug to rush into the classroom in the middle
of a lecture. There would be a fight, the police would be
called and the troublemaker removed. Then the students
would be asked to recount what had happened. Each
would tell a different tale; some would even insist that
there had been not one thug but two. Hence, the professor
would explain, the Russian saying: "He lies like an
eyewitness."

That encounter in Moscow underlines the difficulty most
people find in actually observing what is in front of them,
even when it is obviously physical. The difference arises
partly from a kind of distractedness or inattentiveness in
most of us most of the time. Witnessing events, observing
reality, actually being in touch with what is all around us,

are clearly more complicated activities than many of us realize. Most of us seem to suffer from a limitation of vision, a difficulty in seeing or really contemplating what is before us. This may be partly because we are over-stimulated today and suffer from perceptual overload. We are continually bombarded with carefully crafted electronic images, so that our normal inattentiveness is combined with visual fatigue, and images have to leap out at us and overpower us before they capture our attention. In the universe of the three-minute video clip and fifty-second sound byte, detail is wiped out, subtlety is effaced.

The difficulty we experience in observing reality, in getting in touch with what is beyond ourselves, is further complicated by an innate tendency to change or distort what is in front of us, because of factors, often unconscious and unacknowledged, in our own inner life. Seeing what is in front of us is difficult enough, but it is made more difficult when we get in our own way and project our own inner turmoil on to external reality. Projections of this sort happen all the time, even to comparatively uncomplicated people. But many of us have complex inner natures and we project our tensions, angers and anxieties on to external reality, on to other people, and they bounce impressions back towards us of threat, hostility or rejection. Most human beings are comparatively unknowing about themselves; some are almost completely ignorant about their own drives and motivations, unexplored and unadmitted assumptions, and even the effect they have upon other people. Modern psychological insights have shown us how much of our own nature and its impulses are hidden deep within our unconscious mind; and how often our behaviour is dictated by factors in our past or from within the recesses of our own psyche that we do not acknowledge.

Another King

The things we denounce most passionately in others are often things we are afraid of in ourselves, and the parts of our nature we keep repressed and unacknowledged are often genuine parts of our own personality that we have refused to give scope to, because we have been taught, however unconsciously, to be ashamed of them. And they take their revenge in many ways. Sometimes they erupt irrationally into life and we do something really crazy or out of character. Most often the effort of keeping them out of the living room and down in the cellar adds an edginess and tension to our life, so that we become rather tightly wound people, emotionally frigid, our lives lacking sweep, and recklessness, and generosity. We spend so much time sitting on ourselves that we never learn to relax; but how can we relax when we know that other self is in there somewhere, ready at any moment to jump out and shame us by some gross or unseemly act? I think this is one of the reasons why Jesus liked what some called 'low' company: prostitutes, drunkards, criminals and other outcasts. There was disorder and confusion in their lives but there was no illusion, no pretence. I think this was one of the things he was getting at in the parable of the Prodigal Son. There are three main characters in the story, the father and his two sons, but the *focus* is on the loving constancy of the father. Each of the sons abuses the love of the father, the younger son by going into the far country and wasting his father's gift, the older of the two by a grudging obedience that did the right thing for the wrong reason. Most types of human frailty are contained within the range of behaviour that stretches between the two brothers. The younger son represents the human tendency to excess and destructive self-indulgence, whereas the older son shows a kind of emotional meanness and lack of generosity. Each weakness has its own corresponding strength: profligates are often compassionate and understanding of human weakness, while puritans are usually disciplined and steadfast. In fact, each needs to learn from the other, the prodigal learning something about endurance and obedience from his older brother, while he, in turn, needs to capture something of the openness and daring that characterized the younger man. Each gets his relationship with his father wrong. The wild young man pushes his father's love for him to the ultimate test, while his sober and steadfast brother seems to have no sense of that love and its graciousness, seeing everything in contractual terms with nothing of the freedom and generosity and imprudence of real love. We think we know this story too well, but it is good from time to time to read it with care:

There was a man who had two sons; and the younger of them said to his father, "Father, give me the share of property that falls to me." And he divided his living between them. Not many days later, the younger son gathered all he had and took his journey into a far country, and there he squandered his property in loose living. And when he had spent everything, a great famine arose in that country, and he began to be in want . . .

And he arose and came to his father. But while he was yet at a distance, his father saw him and had compassion, and ran and embraced him and kissed him. And his son said to him, "Father, I have sinned against heaven and before you; I am no longer worthy to be called your son." But the father said to his servants, "Bring quickly the best robe, and put it on him; and put a ring on his hand, and shoes on his feet; and bring the fatted calf and kill it, and let us eat and make merry; for this my son was dead, and is alive again; he was lost, and is found." And they began to make merry.

Now his elder son was in the field; and he came and drew near to the house, he heard music and dancing . . .

But he was angry and refused to go in. His father came out and entreated him, but he answered his father, "Lo, these many years I have served you, and I never disobeyed your command; yet you never gave me a kid, that I might make merry with my friends. But when this son of yours came, who has devoured your living with harlots, you killed for him the fatted calf!" And he said to him, "Son, you are always with me, and all that is mine is yours. It was fitting to make merry and be glad, for this your brother was dead, and is alive; he was lost, and is found." (Luke 15:11–14,20–24,25,28–32)

Each son had to learn a wonderful and liberating lesson about the father's love: it is constant and unwavering and needs only to be turned to. The younger son "came to himself" and went home to his father's arms, and the older brother's complaint was heard and replied to with disarming graciousness. The prodigal son and his brother were both humbled by the kindness and mercy of their father, so unlike their own self-absorption. The story ends with the father's gentle admonition to his first-born son, but there is no reason why we should not go on to add a final scene of our own, in which the two brothers unite in gratitude and admiration of their father, forgetting their own conflicts and failures in sheer thankfulness.

This is, on one level, a parable about personal integration, about getting in touch with the different parts of our own nature. We have to befriend each part, the younger brother and the older brother, and acknowledge their different needs. But in most of us there is confusion rather than integration. Human beings are rarely whole and balanced creatures, so it is not surprising that their hold on or perceptions of reality are limited or selective, rather than rounded and complete. Some of this has to do with concentrating on bits of reality and excluding others. We all know, for instance, the type of person, often an academic of some sort, who is closely in touch with some branch of external reality, such as history or theology, philosophy or science, but who is emotionally illiterate, deeply oblivious of his or her own nature and its working and the effect it has on others. The intelligent, the clever, are not always wise in their relationships, in their ability to understand the fears and weaknesses, the loves and longings of others. Wisdom is a rare kind of balance of the personality that enables it to be in touch with reality in its various forms – internal, as well as external, and even that ultimate reality we think of as the mystery of God.

What all this seems to show is that reality and our perceptions of it are far from straightforward. Far from things being simple, the universe, external as well as internal reality, is like a hall of mirrors in which strange distortions appear: vast dropsical balloons of inflated opinion; the crazy elongated deformations of prejudice and hatred; and the squat compressions of cynicism and negativity.

Now it must be obvious that if we experience such difficulty in seeing what is presented to our *physical* senses and in knowing our own nature and its springs and forces, then it will be even more difficult to be attentive to the *spiritual* reality, which religion claims is also in front of us. If we do not always correctly observe our neighbour or ourselves whom we frequently see, how can we be aware of the God whom we cannot see? Getting in touch with external reality, as well as with the reality of our own inner life, requires careful attention and a kind of reverence towards the thing that is before us. It is egotism that seems to distort our picture of reality, and by egotism I mean the overweening intrusion of and pre-occupation with the self. And egotism does not come only in the form of inflated conceit and lack of real interest in other people. We can be equally preoccupied with our own inadequacy, our own guilts and fears, in a way that distorts and hinders our ability to get in touch with what's outside ourselves.

Modern approaches to counselling and psychotherapy have taught us much about all this. People who volunteer as counsellors to people in need, have to learn, above all and first of all, to *listen*. And this listening is not a passive and vacant thing. It is very costly, because it calls for the listener to empty himself or herself of prejudices, fears and preconceptions, so that the self will not intrude upon the other person whose story is being told. Such non-judgemental listening, without invading the other person's integrity, is the most basic element in building up relationships of trust, therapeutic relationships, sharing and helping relationships. People who cannot listen are not able to help others, because they get themselves in the way of the other person's story, they intrude their own reality into the other person's difficulties in inappropriate ways. *Real* listening is a parable of our approach to the divine mystery, the mystery of ultimate reality. If it is easy to get ourselves and external reality wrong, it must be much easier to get the search for ultimate meaning and value wrong. The mistakes seem to come in two forms. We can make God in our own image by projecting our own needs or preoccupations on to the mystery that confronts us, and back it bounces a picture of ourselves, a God who corresponds in minute particulars to our own weakness and littleness, hating what we hate, confirming our own fantasies and fears. We end up worshipping or fearing some version of ourselves. Our religion becomes a neurosis, a device that keeps us from facing reality, a technique that keeps us from encountering the real mystery of God.

Much religion is pathological, but so is much avoidance of religion, and that is the second mistake we can make. The rejection of religion can be a rejection of responsibility, a refusal to live seriously, to address the big issues. We may refuse to seek the ultimate meaning and purpose in life because it may challenge our selfishness; it may make demands upon us, it may call us to moral and spiritual non-conformity in a conformist society; it may present us with goals that conflict with our own ambitions and those whose approval we seek. It seems to be the case that spiritual reality lets us do all this, because it can only be discovered and loved freely. But though it will not coerce us, it will never leave us alone; it will always be a voice beneath the voices that we hear, a tug at our coat sleeves, a sudden yearning for something we cannot even express. One of the greatest and most troubled intellects of human history knew all this from inside his own experience. He spent years avoiding his encounter with that ultimate reality we call God and later, when he had made his peace with it, he wrote these famous words: "God, you have made us for yourself and our hearts are restless till they rest in you."[1]

And, though it may sound strange, it is resting that we must learn to do. We must achieve a kind of relaxed

42

attentiveness, so that we can open ourselves towards the mystery. The mystery has not left itself without witnesses, or direction signs, for those who truly seek it. It is important to make a distinction here between religion and God, between the spiritual mystery we seek and the human traditions we inherit from those who have sought it before us. If God is that other country, that mysterious reality we yearn for, then religious traditions are like maps. They are not the country, they are only the maps; but any searcher, any wanderer in that country, would be unwise to travel without the guidance of those who have gone before, to go out without the map, without some knowledge of the terrain. This is one of the functions of what we call in religion 'holy scriptures'. Scripture, sacred writing, is the gathered tradition of God's encounter with humanity down the centuries. It's a kind of map of the mystery of God, or a log book of the experience men and women have had in their journeys into that mystery. On one level, of course, it is a series of historical documents, many of which relate to specific historical events no longer recoverable by us. And it can be studied on that level as history, as text, but its spiritual use is primordial. This is its living use – a means of approach to the mystery we seek.

If we enter its world the Bible will introduce us to the landscape of our own soul. This is part of what we mean when we say that the Bible has authority. It has a power, when meditated on, to interpret the meaning of our existence to us and bring us up against the mystery we call God. The Bible offers us a series of events or stories that connect with or make sense of our own private story. All the events that are used in this way began as real history, though the historical core may now be obscure and to a very great extent unrecoverable. But something important has happened to these stories that has lifted them from time past into a dramatic, living present, making them usable by us, as they have been used before us and will continue to be used after us. It is hard to describe in theory or in abstract terms what has happened to these stories, or how they can be used by us today. Some things, indeed many of the important and quirky things in life, cannot be translated. There are no apt or perfect verbal equivalents for them. The moment when you first find your balance and are actually riding a bike is one of those moments; so is swimming for the first time, or hang gliding, or beginning to think in a foreign language. The experience comes only with the experience, the meaning is found *within* and not outside the experience.

I want now to look at some parts of that record and try to enter into their meaning for our life today.

In the sixth month the angel Gabriel was sent from God to a city of Galilee named Nazareth, to a virgin betrothed to a man whose name was Joseph, of the house of David; and the virgin's name was Mary. And he came to her and said, "Hail, O favoured one, the Lord is with you!" But she was greatly troubled at the saying, and considered in her mind what sort of greeting this might be. And the angel said to her, "Do not be afraid, Mary, for you have found favour with God. And behold, you will conceive in your womb and bear a son, and you shall call his name Jesus" . . .

And Mary said to the angel, "How shall this be, since I have no husband?" And the angel said to her, "The Holy Spirit will come upon you, and the power of the Most High will overshadow you; therefore the child to be born will be called holy, the Son of God." . . .

44

And Mary said, "Behold, I am the handmaid of the Lord; let it be to me according to your word." And the angel departed from her. (Luke 1:26–31,34–5,38)

Then Herod summoned the wise men secretly and ascertained from them what time the star appeared; and he sent them to Bethlehem, saying, "Go and search diligently for the child, and when you have found him bring me the word, that I too may come and worship him." When they had heard the king they went their way; and lo, the star which they had seen in the East went before them, till it came to rest over the place where the child was . . .

And being warned in a dream not to return to Herod, they departed to their own country by another way . . .

Then Herod, when he saw that he had been tricked by the wise men, was in a furious rage, and he sent and killed all the male children in Bethlehem and in all that region who were two years old or under, according to the time which he had ascertained from the wise men. (Matthew 2:7–9,12,16)

These stories are either about how God comes to us, or about our approach to the people and places God has come to. They are also about holiness, which is the name we give to that quality of "otherness", that quality of 'God is present here', that we find in certain people and even in certain places. When we come by night to the holy place we are seeking, we find it very quiet and unregarded, strangely powerless, troubling. The real epiphanies and the most significant and effective annunciations come to the secret people, the quiet people, the ones who are and largely remain unknown. What they all have in common, though, is an ability to listen, wait and obey, without surprise. They do not seem to get in their own way or in the way of what is being show to them. There is very little point in haggling over the exact history of these encounters with the divine, for if we want to learn, we have to *enter* that world and be quiet before it. Its meaning is *inside* not outside, and this, of course, is the great Catch 22 of all religious experience and spiritual reality. We cannot really get an independent handle on it from outside, a watertight explanation, a sort of royal commission report into its complexities, produced with judicious objectivity. If we attempt that, all we shall get is a series of still photographs of a bafflingly intricate ballet; or it will be like looking through a telescope at someone on the telephone, not hearing the voice but seeing the lips move; but religion's meaning is *inside* its structure not outside, which is why it remains bafflingly and infuriatingly unresolved. It is simply *there* and if we would understand, we must first believe. If we would see the inside, we must first enter, and that seems to be the difficulty.

Mysteriously, however, many in every generation (and some of them acute and interesting people) make that strange submission and go into that quiet world; and when they do they find at the heart of it a silence and a waiting; they meet quiet people, like Mary, who hear voices and see visions, without fuss and with no self-advertisement. The whole thing seems to turn conventional values upside down and inside out, a theme which appears repeatedly in the Christian tradition: but here the theme does seem to be about hiddenness and simplicity. The contrasts are all between glittering, mighty and opinionated people, who are enormously insecure, such as Herod, and the coming of a divine mystery to the obscure and the unregarded, such as Mary and Joseph and the shepherds, abiding in the fields. These are ancient contrasts, but they are still powerful and challenging, because most of us range ourselves, however unconsciously, with the mighty, certainly in matters of the mind. We want persuasive words of wisdom, convincing arguments and watertight theories, and not this sloppy, mystical, backstreets rumour of some sort of veiled divinity slipping incognito into history, with such an unconvincing alibi. It may all be folly and nonsense, of course, but the theme is intriguingly regular when we get to the very heart of pure religion. There seems to be a lack of interest in what we need if we are to be persuaded or impressed. We are not overwhelmed by argument or compelled by superior intellectual power: the whole thing is insultingly obscure and naive. And yet something about it, something there, something worth travelling towards, seems to compel a sort of submission, summoning us to what T.S. Eliot called

> A condition of complete simplicity
> (Costing not less than everything).[2]

And if we get even remotely close to it, it seems to call in question so many of the things that have power over us, including the very important power of reason. We feel drawn, in spite of ourselves, to wait, to rest and to be quiet. Whatever the Virgin Birth was historically or gynaecologically, it does seem to capture something of this elusive paradox of the divine encountering the human, because our predicament is precisely that we can so easily conceive a God out of the stuff of our own mind and fancy, by our own logic and rationality. But what we then humanly conceive is of our flesh and of our mind, an extension of ourselves. It does not finally and profoundly persuade us because we know we can so easily do these things to ourselves; we can make up whole worlds, whole realities. Yet we still have this strange mystery of virginity giving birth.

I am not interested, for the moment, in arguments about miracles and whether God could, would or ought to have come among us in this way. The claim seems to me to be much deeper and more mysterious than that, and far beyond the roundabout arguments we have with each other about the exact status of the virginal conception of Jesus Christ by Mary. It has something to do with our need for God to fill us, our need for otherness, our need to recognize the approach of God. How can we conceive the life of God in our hearts unaided? That was Mary's question to the angel: "How can this be? – How can I know God? How can real knowledge of God, real experience of God, be born in my barren life, my bewildered mind?" And yet, if we have the spiritual hunger, we do long for the spirit of the most high to be born within us. We want to conceive the mystery in our own heart, but how can this be?

There is always this wistful incredulity, this disbelieving longing for belief. In spite of ourselves, we long for Emmanuel, we long for God to be with us. Well, at some point, we have to say "yes" to the mystery, make an act of submission – no matter how embarrassing it may be, no matter how firmly it commits us to a kind of social and intellectual illegitimacy. Mary is not a likely example for a world of power and certainty, yet she is the model of faith and that which was born in her was of the Holy Spirit. Faith, after all, is a gift. We cannot conceive it. It cannot be artificially generated, it can only be received, though it may be longed for, wept for, grieved after. It is always something that comes to us from that other place and bears its own testimony within it. And there is no set term for its conception. For some it takes a lifetime to say "yes", while others are able to say "yes" for a whole lifetime. Some are like old Simeon, in Luke's Gospel, whose eyes saw his salvation only as he himself was about to depart, while others see it with the clear eyes of youth. For faith *is* a gift. Gifts can be refused, but they cannot be compelled: yet we have to say "yes" to a gift. I know many people who long to, but cannot, believe. And I say to them all that they must wait, be gentle with themselves and towards the divine mystery. If you have little or no faith, but long for it to be born in you, don't fret about it or struggle with it. Gifts cannot be demanded. Learn to wait. Practise quietness. And make yourself *small*. This is difficult for those of us who are proud, especially if we are clever as well as proud. But there is no other way. To enter the stable at Bethlehem you have to stoop.

All of that is what we mean by praying. For praying is not about words, or the sound of the voice; it is not about what Jesus called "heaping up empty phrases". Walter Pater claimed that all art constantly aspires towards the condition of music. Well, all genuine prayer aspires towards the condition of silence; and those who cannot keep silence are unlikely to let God really lay hold of their lives. There is a great deal of chatterbox religion that prattles to and about God, yet the really holy seem to sink even further into a kind of eloquent silence that is wordless yet profoundly informing. There is not enough silence in our world and our lives. I dare say someone cleverer than I could work out some mathematical formula that showed how the increased volume and prevalence of noise in our society is in inverse proportion to the sense of transcendence. If the mystery of God is heard in silence, then it would seem to follow that the noisier society becomes, the more noises there are in our own heads and hearts, the less attentive we will be to the whisper of God.

Apart from the thoughts of God being thought through us, we cannot even think our *own* thoughts in this world of wall-to-wall noise. Even the churches are part of it: services going literally with a bang, clergy talking, always talking, and all the restless stir of what E.M. Forster called "poor little talkative Christianity". That is why I like a story that is told of St Francis of Assisi. When he sent his friars out to the villages and cities of his world he told them, "Preach the gospel everywhere; if necessary, use words."

But there *are* quiet places and quiet people, and there is a kind of counter-insurgency, a silence arising in the Church: there are places to go where silence is taken seriously, where people can guide us into its dangers, because, of course, we meet not only God in silence, but *ourselves*. As we go deeper into the mystery of God, we will find that it is absolute, unconditional graciousness; but we have to prepare our lives for that presence, not because God is a demanding guest but because we cannot live with him except on the basis of honesty with and about ourselves. Silence and honesty seem to be pre-conditions for the birth of the mystery of God in our hearts. Most of us bury or repress the sad and lonely and ugly side of ourselves from ourselves. Our weaknesses and needs, our strange hungers and insecurities can lead us to exploit others and indulge ourselves. All of this lovingly angers God, because it damages us. God's pleading for our honesty is for our sake. It is so easy to get the moral side of religion the wrong way round. But clear it all away – forget the moralisms, the commandments, the ordinances, the taboos, the ritualized prohibitions; forget all the structures, all the apparatus of morality and respectability, and try to see with a pure heart the mystery of a God who is incandescent kindness, burningly glorious, full of grace and forgiveness, and you'll understand where it all comes from. God calls us to holiness; not respectability or moral cautiousness, but a kind of helpless surrender to a tremendous lover, who does not want us to perish by sinking into our own unhappy selfishness.

Silence and honesty: we must practise both, though we will never perfect them in this life. Increasingly, we should try to build into our lives little enclosures of silence and regular acts of self-awareness, self-knowledge, self-examination, either in our own solitude or with the help of some friend in the faith, because we rarely see ourselves absolutely straight. We're usually both too hard on ourselves and too soft on ourselves. As we look towards the other country and seek to hear the other king, let us be silent, and in the silence let us own the truth about ourselves.

3

REJECTION

And when they came to the place which
is called The Skull, there they crucified
him, and the criminals, one on the right
and one on the left. (Luke 23:33)

It is usually the first thing I look for on coming into a strange
town. If it's a small country town, the church with its
surrounding graveyard is often on the outskirts, and it is
in the churchyard that I usually expect to find it, though
sometimes it's in the market place or just outside the town
hall. It can vary in design, but there is one type in particular
that I like, because it evokes the waste and pity of war with
a sort of quiet eloquence. The one that stays in my mind
is the statue of a young soldier in World War I uniform,
with head bowed, leaning on his reversed rifle. Invariably
some words that Laurence Binyon wrote are inscribed on
the plinth on which the soldier stands, and round the words
we see the names of the war dead of whom it is written:

They shall grow not old, as we that are left grow old:
Age shall not weary them, nor the years condemn.
At the going down of the sun and in the morning
We will remember them.[1]

All war is waste, even though the waste is often transfigured

by the terrible beauty of heroism, but the war that haunts
the imagination and captures both the misery and majesty
of all that dying is World War I. There is hardly a village
or hamlet in Britain that does not have its memorial to those
who died in that conflict and if we travel the country and
look at them we capture something of the sweep and sorrow
of it. Human beings, especially men, have spent a lot of time
in history killing each other. There are occasions when great
evil has to be opposed, even unto death, but violent human
conflict rarely has that kind of clarity. Most of it has to do
with muddle and vanity and lack of imagination. And men
in particular seem to suffer from a specifically masculine type
of insecurity that makes it difficult for them to back down
or admit they got something wrong. This is what makes
conflict so dangerous between men: the issue of truth or
territory soon gets lost in threats to the ego or male pride
and the protagonists fight till one of them conquers. So there
grows up in history the assumption that subtle things like
ideas or theories, all the complicated things that human
beings disagree about, have to be settled like prize fights
in which the winner takes all. There is a saying which comes,
I think, from the Native American community: "Do not
judge a man until you have spent two weeks walking in his
moccasins." But most us cannot achieve that level of
magnanimity. We are insecure people, unsure of ourselves
deep down, so we defend ourselves and our ideas with a
sort of bristling touchiness that can easily lead to violent
disagreement. We are in permanent conflict within and
between ourselves. And, for me, the most moving and
eloquent symbol of that conflict and its cost is the war
memorial from World War I.

At the heart of human conflict and struggle for power is

insecurity and the fight to survive, to beat off the dangers that lurk around us. We can understand how things would develop like that in a universe in which only the fit survive, and the weak perish. In such a world there will be an almost instinctive worship of strength, power, the ability to compete and win, to get to the top, to protect one's family, clan or little piece of territory. We can all laugh and sneer at the more absurd manifestations of this in the macho, muscle-bound, brawling male, asserting his domination by brute force. But there are other ways of expressing the same instinct. Many people who are physically cowardly are positive bullies in argument and debate, flattening everything in front of them with superior intellectual fire-power, withering the opposition with sarcasm. And a part of us admires all that. Our political system in Britain is to a very great extent based upon this very phenomenon. Parliament, in one of its roles, though it is somewhat diminished today, is a gladiatorial combat zone between political adversaries; and some of the most memorable epochs in parliamentary history featured great combatants who debated with each other fiercely, such as Gladstone and Disraeli, Churchill and Bevan, who fought epic battles. Of course, good debaters have to assemble facts and marshall arguments, but in this kind of arena it helps if they can find the glittering insult, the shimmering barb of invective. Parliament is a primitive and Darwinian place. We have only to listen to Prime Minister's Question Time to realize that.

It is the way of the world and it provides us with spectacle, drama, amusement, exhilaration. It certainly provides the staple diet for many of our entertainments; and for the strong or the merely competent it provides a possible game plan for life. But behind it there often lies insecurity and fear.

Rejection

It is well known that many of the men and women who are most interested in and successful at acquiring wealth and power are insecure people, struggling to gain acceptance, approval, admiration and love from demanding or rejecting parents. They heap up riches and win a kind of admiration from the world, but they rarely assuage the original lonely impulse. Many tycoons who dominate the headlines with their takeovers and compulsive gathering of wealth and power, are emotionally and spiritually impoverished people with little inner life.

Human motivation is notoriously complex, but what often does seem to drive human beings in their pursuit of fame and fortune in life is *precisely* insecurity, the gap caused by the lack of early love, which is transposed into the pursuit of concrete achievements that do not really fill the souls of those who crave them. The spectacle provided by this unguided search for security is endless and fascinating; it provides us with many of the great themes and even some of the pleasures and glories of human history. Yet in the end there is something profoundly slippery and unsatisfying about all of it, which is why the really wealthy go on heaping up riches beyond the point of sanity; and why for all of us there is always another river to cross in our search for the contented place.

We find exactly the same struggles and insecurities among the followers of Jesus, both then and now. The main statement is found in Mark 10:35–45:

> And James and John, the sons of Zebedee, came forward to him, and said to him, "Teacher, we want you to do for us whatever we ask of you." And he said to them, "What do you want me to do for you?" And they said

55

to him, "Grant us to sit, one at your right hand and one at your left, in your glory." But Jesus said to them, "You do not know what you are asking. Are you able to drink the cup that I drink, or to be baptized with the baptism with which I am baptized?" And they said to him, "We are able." And Jesus said to them, "The cup that I drink you will drink; and with the baptism with which I am baptized, you will be baptized; but to sit at my right hand or at my left is not mine to grant, but it is for those for whom it has been prepared."

And when the ten heard it, they began to be indignant at James and John. And Jesus called them to him and said to them, "You know that those who are supposed to rule over the Gentiles lord it over them, and their great men exercise authority over them. But it shall not be so among you; but whoever would be great among you must be your servant, and whoever would be first among you must be slave of all. For the Son of man also came not to be served but to serve, and to give his life as a ransom for many."

Here Jesus acknowledges that the search for power and domination is the way of the world and its organized institutions. "But", he says, "it shall not be so among you."

This theme in the teaching and ministry of Christ points to an extraordinary paradox. It implies that the very ground of reality, the energy that created nature, is a kind of un-force or un-power; it says that the great creator God is not a controlling or overpowering reality, but that the nature of his being is the generous, self-emptying empowerment of others. The very words of creation, "Let there be", are not sensed as imperious commands but as a joyous *sharing* in the love that is the very nature and mystery of God. "*Let there be*, let our love be expressed and shown forth, let us empty ourselves, let us go forth from ourselves and share the mystery of life." This great act of generosity contains the seeds of its own crucifixion, its own rejection, because those who live this way and organize their lives according to this principle must live with the possibility of the rejection of that offering, that sharing, that giving. We are close here to the heart of the great mystery of evil and suffering, which is the reality that most powerfully opposes the affirmation of the mystery of God. The apparent moral neutrality of the universe, its mechanistic coldness, its pain, its indifference to death, torment, tumult, famine, pestilence, earthquake and disaster, speak to some only of an entirely natural process, and any meaning it has is only what we impose upon it in the brief span of our own private life. There is honesty in that view and it is certainly one of the great choices, one of the great assumptions or faiths available to us. Indeed, facts very often seem to be on its side, which is why believers who are impatient with mystery and cannot live with uncertainty often resort to sub-moral justifications for the existence of sorrow and pain, by asserting that all tragedy is explicable either as a school of fortitude or as a punishment for sin. These explanations create a God who seems to be less attractive than an ordinary, kindly human being. They remind me of something Goethe said: "Distrust all those in whom the urge to punish is strong." We must not go down that route. We are enveloped in mystery here and we must not claim an absolutely exact theological confidence in discussing these things. What we get is not a key to the moral riddle of the universe but vision, poetry; and as W.H. Auden said, "Poetry makes nothing happen." Yet poetry may suddenly throw light on the meaning of things, give the visionary glimpse that helps us go round corners and straighten out puzzles and find the courage to endure. The greatest vision of all is this strange picture Christ gives us of the helplessly loving God who lets be, who does not control, grasp or dictate; who lets the universe be and lets us be. This is a theme that runs through scripture like golden and crimson threads amongst all the other themes. John tells us that the mystery of God constantly comes to his own but his own do not receive it.

> He was in the world, and the world was made through him, yet the world knew him not. He came to his own home, and his own people received him not. (John 1:10–11)

And Paul tells us in a strange, passionate and almost inarticulately convincing meditation that God does not try to persuade us with logic or wisdom, but resorts instead to the powerlessness, the folly of the crucifixion.

> Where is the wise man? Where is the scribe? Where is the debater of this age? Has not God made foolish the wisdom of the world? For since, in the wisdom of God, the world did not know God through wisdom, it pleased God through the folly of what we preach to save those who believe. For Jews demand signs and Greeks seek wisdom, but we preach Christ crucified, a stumbling block to Jews and folly to Gentiles, but to those who are called, both Jews and Greeks, Christ the power of God and the wisdom of God. For the foolishness of God is wiser than men, and the weakness of God is stronger than men. (1 Corinthians 1:20–25)

We see the same theme in the life of Christ who refuses to resort to religious power tricks that will influence or persuade people. This is the meaning of the narrative of the temptation in the wilderness where Christ refuses to develop the techniques used by an American television evangelist to manipulate people into his kingdom. The same is true of his reluctance to perform miracles. The miracles of Christ are squeezed out of him by anguish and compassion for the afflicted, not presented as arguments or proofs. For John they reveal a glory that is known not by overwhelming majesty and power, but by a kind of secret pity and beseeching. And the same themes of *letting be*, of non-control, un-force, seem powerfully at work in the crucifixion of Jesus.

At the heart of it is the claim the vision, the sudden poetic recognition that this man of sorrows is God with us, the God who lets be, who does not grasp; that he is the divine power that empties itself; that he is the God who, in Paul's language, though he is rich becomes poor; that the God whom the New Testament celebrates in all these extraordinary paradoxes of emptying and stripping of glory, is among us. The mystery of Christ's divinity in humanity is often talked about by Christians in a kind of fairy-tale language: the rich prince who comes searching for his bride among the poor and disguises himself as a beggar; or even Christ as a kind of undercover cop, disguising himself as human in order to confuse the king of the underworld and destroy his kingdom from within. Analogies like that all suggest that the poverty and the powerlessness of Christ are temporary tactics adopted as expedients. But the reality seems to be more radical than that, according to the New Testament. Christ's abnegation of power, in taking the form of the slave, reveals the very nature of God as ungrasping and self-emptying. The very opposite, in fact, of our insecure attitude to life that forces us to want to be in control. What Christ seeks to show us by parable and example is the nature and being of God. We can only talk of it in negatives, in reversals, in negations of human characteristics, and we make it sound like weakness, like a kind of passivity; and this is why we fall for these analogies that see the self-emptying of God in Christ as a temporary expedient, a momentary disguise, and not his true nature. *Our* God has to be a God of power and might because power and might are our gods, which is why it is very difficult to hear or understand what Christ means.

Christians often turn the cross around, they make it into a sword, they use it as an instrument of power, an instrument of opposition, and they even fight each other over its meaning. And that is the keenest irony in history, because the heart of the Christian message as lived and died by Christ is the reversal and abnegation of power. It is easy to remember the many ways in which Christians have quite literally taken up the sword against each other, slaughtered each other; or taken up the sword against so-called enemies of Christ, such as people of other religions or of none. In a sense the target doesn't matter here. What matters is the reversal of the meaning of Christ and his cross. And, indeed, it is a very difficult meaning to live with, to practise, even to understand, because so much seems to count against it.

So this man of sorrows, who is silent before his accusers, who lifts no finger against his attackers, who refuses to let his followers defend him and who dies one of the most loathsome and cruel deaths ever invented by the sadistic imagination of humanity, becomes a symbol of oppression and an instrument of control The story of the crucifixion is wrenching enough at any level. Even those who do not see any godhead veiled there have to veil their eyes from the awful sorrow and majesty of it; a sorrow that continues to haunt the imagination and provide some of the great human themes: the theme of the rejected friend, the rejected hero; the constant human theme of treason and betrayal, painted in the figure of Judas; the theme of infidelity and disloyalty portrayed by the tragic, broken-hearted Peter, and the craven disciples who forsake him and flee away from him. All of that continues to exert an extraordinary and irresistible appeal to musicians and artists, as though it tapped into some great root in our own unconscious nature; as though it were a great and permanent human reality into which we plug our imagination; as though it were one of the great underground rivers of what Jung called "the collective unconscious".

The theme, of course, is there in many cultures in many different ways and it constantly seems to echo in human experience. But for those with the eye of faith, the faith that befriends ordinary intelligence, ordinary outward sense, the spectacle is even more harrowing and amazing, because it discloses to us not only the sadistic execution of a courageous and attractive man of religious genius, but the very death of God. It demonstrates the acceptance by God of the logical conclusion of his own nature as letting be, as un-force, as ungrasping, self-emptying, beseechingness. There are no words that capture the reality, so we are forced to create words or negate words or pile up phrases in order to capture the sublime enormity of it. The heart of the message is that our strange tormented universe, born in violence and explosive power, a universe that preys upon itself and devours itself; that this universe and the laws, philosophies and logic of power that it throws up, are a great misshapen version of the original vision of *letting be*, of generosity and sharing. In little ways we know this from the experience of our own lives. We can remember, if we have ever been in positions of authority of any sort, how difficult it is to *let people be*, to give them control, to give them power, even to give them a job and let them get on with it. There are many examples of that paradox, that proverbial human difficulty. It's the stuff of legend and myth; of all family disputes, all office quarrels, all high table rivalries, or intercollegiate feuds. It's the story of a universe that is somehow out of control and yet is *in* to control, a universe that is insecure and avoiding death, and yet seeks to avoid death by the logic of control, the logic of the coffin. It is not a free universe, not a universe of letting be, of self-effacing freeing of people to be themselves, to discover themselves, but a controlling, overpowering universe. Not utterly so, of course; in the language of the old theologians, it is not utterly corrupt, not beyond redemption, and still contains strange echoes of that primordial reality in God which is generous self-giving mutuality and love. There are elements of that in those who give up their lives for others and even in those who know they should not control others, even though they have a lust to control. Indeed, we could not recognize the vision that comes from Christ if we were not, even now, in some sense, citizens of that other country and subjects of that other king. It is part of the tragedy that we partly know these things, partly live them, and yet are in constant rebellion against them, against our own best joy, our own best happiness. We so often destroy the things we love, including our own heart's peace.

Rejection

The crucifixion speaks poignantly of things in our own life, ways in which we run from our own best good, ways in which we exploit, strip others, gloat upon them, abuse and control them. Partly because of the limits of our vocabulary and partly because of the very psychology of power itself, we fail to capture the dynamic nature of the paradox of God's abnegation of power. We talk about it inevitably as *powerlessness*, as essentially an absence of something, a denial of something, even though it may be something evil. But that does not actually capture the positive and dynamic nature of God's life as generous self-giving. There's nothing supine or passive about this, any more than there's anything passive about a great fountain that pours pure water into a desert that blossoms like a rose, though the fountain is constantly giving out and not taking in. We are crucified by our own linguistic inadequacy here, which is why there is a whole tradition of speech about God in negatives and a whole tradition of spirituality that follows the same way, echoed in T.S. Eliot's famous passage from *East Coker*:

I said to my soul be still, and wait without hope
For hope would be hope for the wrong thing; wait without
     love
For love would be love of the wrong thing; there is yet faith
But the faith and the love and the hope are all in the waiting.
Wait without thought, for you are not ready for thought:
So the darkness shall be the light, and the stillness the
     dancing.[2]

But what is at stake here is not our ability to get a description down on paper or into our minds of this metaphysical conundrum of the creative energy of the universe holding itself in the repose of generous self-effacement, but that we open ourselves to the reality of the experience and let it be born in us, let it happen in our lives, become part of that utterly revolutionary energy of the kingdom of God, become naturalized citizens, adopted sons and daughters of that other country, allowing its ethos to envelop and change us. And this ethos is holiness, gentleness, self-control, and above all, generosity and kindness. We recognize the citizens of that other country, because they are not out to manipulate us, recruit us for their cause, get us into their card index system or on to their ecclesiastical filofax. We know them, because while something about them may challenge us to the very root of our being and fill us with shame and a deep longing, they also *affirm* us, they are generous towards us, they give us a sense of absolute acceptance. Only if we are wrapped in layers of self-deception, hypocrisy, phoniness and pride, are they likely to enrage us; but if we come to them seeking and open, however wounded we are, however saddened by the knowledge of our own flaws and frailties, however driven by our own doubts and confusions – when we come to them we will find acceptance and no blackmail, no pressure. We shall find a gracious silence. And this is what we need.

One of the things we have learned from some of the best modern psycho-therapeutic techniques is that the person with the difficulty has to be accepted and affirmed absolutely. Insecure people are constantly testing and manipulating others, pushing them to the point of rejection, so that their own sense of self-loathing will be confirmed. That is why the counsellor or therapist has to offer unconditional love and acceptance of the person. But this is not a modern discovery − it is the very *heart* of the Christian message. In the crucifixion of Jesus, God shows us that he will not repudiate or reject us. True to the logic of his own nature as love-that-will-not-control, he endures everything we do to him. He won't play our game and lose his temper or loose a thunderbolt at us, finally confirming our own self-loathing by rejecting us as ultimately unlovable. The contrary is true: he allows us to test his love to destruction, thereby giving us the absolute assurance of his love and understanding and forgiveness. He saves us from self-destruction by staying with us through all our moral tantrums, all our self-hating denials of goodness, all our spiritual wanderings, all our betrayals, until his unlimited love breaks our heart and makes us smile. No one has put it better than Austin Farrer:

> God forgives me with the compassion of his eyes, but my back is turned to him. I have been told that he forgives me, but I will not turn and have the forgiveness, not though I feel the eyes on my back. God forgives me, for he takes my head between his hands and turns my face to his to make me smile at him. And though I struggle and hurt those hands − for they are human, though divine, human and scarred with nails − though I hurt them, they do not let go until he has smiled me into smiling; and that is the forgiveness of God.[3]

What Christ did was to announce the presence even now of that limitless love in the midst of history and its rack and ruin. He came to inaugurate a new kind of creation, to build a community of men and women who would live as though that other country, that other kingdom, already *were*. And the things that Christ said about that other country which he called "the kingdom of heaven" all hark back to visionary passages of great longing and beauty from the Old Testament which picture a contented, balanced community in which tragedy is purged, the lion lies down with the lamb, all oppression ceases, earthquake, famine and pestilence are banished from the earth and children play endlessly in the streets of the holy city. Here are a few of these bewitching prophecies:

The wilderness and the dry land shall be glad, the desert shall rejoice and blossom. (Isaiah 35:1)

They shall come and sing aloud on the height of Zion, and they shall be radiant over the goodness of the Lord, over the grain, the wine, and the oil, and over the young of the flock and the herd; their life shall be like a watered garden, and they shall languish no more. (Jeremiah 31:12)

Then the nations that are left round about you shall know that I, the Lord, have rebuilt the ruined places, and replanted that which was desolate; I, the Lord, have spoken, and I will do it. (Ezekiel 36:36)

"Behold, the days are coming," says the Lord, "when the ploughman shall overtake the reaper and the treader of grapes him who sows the seed; the mountain shall drip sweet wine, and all the hills shall flow with it." (Amos 9:13)

It's a bewitching fantasy, the Messianic longing for the end time, the other country, the land of lost content, somewhere over the rainbow. Does it have any more reality than our fairy tales and legends, our daydreams and longings? Was Christ just another fantasist? Or are these dreams and longings coming from some reality deep within us?

But how can this be? How can we live pretending that lions lie down with lambs when we know they don't? We know that if we send a lamb into a lion's den it will be devoured. If we seek to live the impossible ethic of the Beatitudes we'll be trampled on. And yet, if we believe Christ when he tells us that the kingdom is near us, at hand, is within us; if we try to live *now* as though that kingdom already were, we shall begin to see it as this world restored, renewed and returned to an original and true design which we sense beneath the distortion which we witness. That original pattern continues to haunt us, that other country continues to call us. It is why we all expect more from relationships than they can bear, and are surprised when they are not perfect and happy. It is why we are always searching for what R.S. Thomas called "The glimpsed good place permanent". It is the world as we know it, somehow purged of sorrow and regret. And Christ is suggesting that these hopeless longings, these Utopian ideals, are coming from a place beyond, a time apart, another country we are born remembering. Jesus invites his followers to live here and now as though they were living in that other country. They are to live according to the mysterious reversals of power in that kingdom, as though it were at one with the kingdoms of this world. This accounts for the strange, passionate, beautiful contradictions of the Beatitudes – blessed are the poor, the mourners, the meek, the hungry, the gentle, the single in heart, the peacemakers, the persecuted, the reviled. In that other country people do not revenge themselves, exploit or control one another, and Jesus calls his disciples to live in that other country, that other kingdom *now*. Because that, apparently, is the eternal and enduring reality.

But we know what kind of visionary absurdity it all is, don't we? We certainly cannot run the world that way and we cannot even run our private lives by that impossible ideal. And yet, something does catch us from time to time, some yearning, some longing that the impossible might be possible, a fleeting recognition to which part of us gives consent. Sometimes in the midst of a flaming row with someone, possibly someone we love, we catch the insanity and irrationality of our posturing and obduracy and a little voice within whispers "peace, and be at peace", and we edge back from the brink. Karl Barth said there could be no ethics without a touch of utopianism, that longing for the good place permanent, the kingdom of heaven, the other country. Without that pulling and tugging at us we settle back and acquiesce in life's sorrow, we put it aside. We get used to the horrors. As Tom Wolfe said of his New York millionaires in his novel *Bonfire of the Vanities*, we try to insulate ourselves from all the wild, sorrowful and tragic people out there. We insulate, build a fortified zone between us and them to keep them at bay, keep sorrow at bay, keep reality away. We insulate. And people who refuse to insulate get trampled on, just like Jesus. That is the other argument against the Jesus fantasy, the other country complex. Look what they did to Jesus, look where it got him! What they did to Jesus is what they always do to people who try to live the Beatitudes. Any mug who turns the other cheek, or tries to make peace or tries to stop a runaway train by holding up his hand in blessing, gets what's coming to him. Look what happened to Jesus!

And this where preaching the cross becomes almost impossible, or impossible for people like me who do not quite live by it. Following Christ is not really a *word* thing, a saying of words or a holding of words in the head; or a commitment to a particular order of words or a certain way of putting them. I have done all that, go on doing it. I have said the words, promised in words. Christian history is suffocated in words, yet how few of those words become flesh. In Christ the Word became flesh and in the Church the Flesh becomes words. That is why preaching becomes a torment for the preacher who is not a saint. How can I in my worldliness summon you to this impossible ideal? How can I, who have not died, call you to give up your lives? It is because I am trapped. In the chapel at King's College, London, there is a cross in the form of a man-trap that has been prised open. And half-Christians like me are usually people who are struggling against the trap of the cross. Like the two jaws of a trap, the cross is ambiguous. It is both consolation and torment. On the one hand, it is the sign of my salvation. It shows me that God has absorbed all my sin, has borne it on his own body, has taken it all away, has turned the other cheek to me, has answered my curses with a blessing, has taken all my rage and lust and anxiety and indifference, and simply absorbed them, soaked them up. And the most unbearable part of it is that he comforts me with those bleeding hands, he consoles me for my grief at murdering him. How can I live with that and not be changed by it, be drawn into that mystery of unconditional love? I want to. I hear Paul:

Have this mind in you which was also in Christ Jesus, who, though he was in the form of God did not count equality with God a thing to be grasped, but emptied himself, taking the form of a servant, being born in the likeness of man. And being found in human form he humbled himself and became obedient unto death, even death on a cross. (Philippians 2:5–8)

So the cross becomes my burden as well as my consolation and I fear what it will do to my life if I ever let it shut upon me. I am lured by its sweetness and terrified by its summons to live according to its logic in the world as it is. Caught as I am in this dilemma, I cannot challenge you to take up what I spend my life circling round. But I can remind us both of what is involved.

The cross forgives my false domination of others, but it calls me to renounce the way of power. The cross absolves me for my constant attempts to insulate myself against the sorrows of the world, yet it summons me to enter the world's sorrow and help bear it. The cross understands my ambitions and insecurity and consoles me in my self-disgust when I try to work the system to my benefit and manipulate others to my good, but it exhorts me to abandon my anxiety and cast myself only upon the strength of God. The cross knows the needs within my nature that lead me to use others to comfort myself and assuage my loneliness, but it challenges me to reverence the sanctity of every child of God. The cross offers me absolute consolation, and in the same moment it calls me to absolute self-surrender.

I know I cannot live without the former; but how can I possibly live with the latter? How can I live and die, be a penitent and an aspirant to holiness, sinner and saint? Words will not resolve that enigma, nor any power of mine. Anyway, I have run out of words, though there is always the silence and the waiting. And the looking – there is always the looking, even though it is from very far away.

In Matthew's account of the crucifixion there is a haunting verse. Just after they have crucified Jesus and raised the cross upright we are told: "And sitting down they watched him there." That is all we can do. We cannot resolve the riddle of the cross as both consolation and challenge, the sign of God's love and the emblem of his demand, by our words or by our own effort. We are stretched across the open trap – but if we sit and look at him the dilemma may be resolved, and the trap of the cross may at last close upon us and maybe we shall discover that the trap does not bite us and impale us. Instead, we may find ourselves entrapped between the bleeding hands of God as he forces us to look at him and smiles us into smiling.

4

RESTORATION

. . . tell his disciples and Peter that he
is going before you into Galilee. (Mark
16:7)

During church services little bits from the Bible are read,
little passages from quite long books. There are perfectly
good reasons for that but it has its drawbacks, because books
are meant to be read as *books* and not just as collections
of spiritual epigrams. That's why it is useful, from time to
time, to read a whole Gospel, say, at a sitting; to read it
as a book to get the full impact and freshness of it. In fact,
there's an even better thing to do, and that is to hear it read
from beginning to end. I am able to do this quite often
because I spend much of my time driving around my diocese,
and as I drive I usually listen to cassettes on my player. From
time to time I listen to a whole Gospel. Some time ago I
had to drive from Edinburgh to a retreat house in
Northumberland, a drive of about two hours. I have a
recording of Mark's Gospel that takes that length of time,
so I played it as I drove down to Shepherd's Dene and I was
struck in a fresh way by the structure and oddness of the
Gospel. While I was at Shepherd's Dene I came across a
sermon by Austin Farrer on Mark's Gospel. With Farrer's
sermon in my mind I drove back to Edinburgh at the end
of the week and listened to the Gospel again, and I want

to share with you the double impact it had on me: the impact of the Gospel itself and the guidance I received from that little sermon by Austin Farrer.

But before we start the trip we ought to enquire about the author of the Gospel, because we can often get a handle on a book if we know something about who wrote it. We cannot really say very much about it, but there's a tradition that is was written by John Mark, a disciple of St Peter and a bit of a failure, certainly as far as St Paul was concerned. There is an intriguing little note in the fourteenth chapter that some people identify as an autobiographical clue, a sort of signature. It occurs just after they have arrested Jesus in the Garden of Gethsemane: "And a young man followed him, with nothing but a linen cloth about his body; and they seized him, but he left the linen cloth and ran away naked" (Mark 14:51,52). If it was written by John Mark, and if he was the young man who fled away naked in the night, then we know something about him. We also know that he failed at a difficult point in his career and was dismissed by the apostle Paul, a man who never suffered fools gladly or really, it seems to me, had sufficient sympathy for the frailty of others. Anyway, in Acts 15:36–40 we read:

After some days Paul said to Barnabas, "Come, let us return and visit the brethren in every city where we proclaimed the word to the Lord, and see how they are." And Barnabas wanted to take with them John called Mark. But Paul thought best not to take with them one who had withdrawn from them in Pamphylia, and had not gone with them to the work. And there arose a sharp contention, so that they separated from each other; Barnabas took Mark with him and sailed away to Cyprus, but Paul chose Silas and departed, being commended by the brethren to the grace of the Lord. (Acts 15:36–40)

Here we have a little snapshot of a follower of Christ who was no hero. And this Gospel is certainly interested in failure and failures. If it was written by John Mark we can understand that interest. But let us turn to it now and look at it. We can conveniently divide it into three parts.

The first part paints a picture of the great compassion of Christ. The motto could come from Mark 1:41 where Jesus heals a leper: "Moved with pity, he stretched out his hand and touched him, and said to him, 'Be clean'." In the first part of the Gospel crowds of sick and needy people follow Christ, because of his great pity and compassion:

Again he began to teach beside the sea. And a very large crowd gathered about him, so that he got into a boat and sat in it on the sea; and the whole crowd was beside the sea on the land. (4:1)

And when Jesus had crossed again in the boat to the other side, a great crowd gathered about him; and he was beside the sea. Then came one of the rulers of the synagogue, Jairus by name; and seeing him, he fell at his feet, and besought him saying, "My little daughter is at the point of death. Come and lay your hands on her, so that she may be made well, and live." And he went with him. (5:21–42)

As I drove through the Borders I wasn't feeling particularly good about myself. I was, in fact, very conscious of the gap between my Christian profession and the quality of my life.

74

In fact, I was a bit self-pitying, wishing I were in a job that seemed more realizable and whose aspirations were more achievable. But listening again to the story of the compassion, the pity of Christ, his healing of the sick, and the way ordinary people followed him in their need, I felt enormously comforted and consoled. I was drawn yet again by the enormous appeal of the compassionate Christ. As I drove through Jedburgh I felt soothed and consoled by the Gospel.

But half-way through the book there is a dramatic change of mood. It comes at the end of the eighth chapter, which is sometimes called 'the hinge of Mark'; it is a call to heroism and crossbearing.

> He began to teach them that the Son of man must suffer many things, and be rejected by the elders and the chief priests and the scribes, and be killed, and after three days rise again. And he said this plainly. And Peter took him, and began to rebuke him. But turning and seeing his disciples, he rebuked Peter, and said, "Get behind me, Satan! For you are not on the side of God, but of men."
>
> And he called to him the multitude with his disciples, and said to them, "If any man would come after me, let him deny himself and take up his cross and follow me. For whoever would save his life will lose it; and whoever loses his life for my sake and the gospel's will save it. For what does it profit a man, to gain the whole world and forfeit his life? For what can a man give in return for his life?" (8:31–37)

From then on Jesus tightens the screws, he raises the demand upon his disciples For instance, he creates the high standard of Christian marriage: "Whoever divorces his wife and marries another, commits adultery against her; and if she divorces her husband and marries another, she commits adultery" (10:11–12). And a few verses further on (10:23ff) he rules out the pursuit of wealth. In these verses he calls us to the great but difficult area of absolute fidelity and to the great vision of austerity and self-denial. This heightening of challenge, this call to heroic self-denial and self-sacrifice, reaches a mysterious climax at the Last Supper. Surrounded by his band of heroes, the glorious company of the apostles, he predicts his own destruction and their desertion:

> And Jesus said to the, "You will all fall away; for it is written, 'I will strike the shepherd, and the sheep will be scattered.' But after I am raised up, I will go before you to Galilee." Peter said to him, "Even though they all fall away, I will not." And Jesus said to him, "Truly, I say to you, this very night, before the cock crows twice, you will deny me three times." But he said vehemently, "If I must die with you, I will not deny you." And they all said the same. (14:27–31)

As I listened to these harrowing words something of the old desire that drew me as a young man to the service of Christ rose in me again; the great call to spiritual heroism, the voice that appeals to the part of us that, in Gerard Manley Hopkins' phrase, "wants war, wants wounds", rang within me as it had rung in the minds and hearts of the apostles. Farrer reminds us that if this were a conventional story, an entertainment, there would be a bold resolution: we would turn the page and see Christ and his band of brothers going bravely to their destiny together. But when we turn this page we read: "And they all forsook him and fled." When we turn this page it is failure and flight we find. In particular, we look mercilessly at the humiliation of the chief of the apostles, our Lord's own lieutenant, Simon Peter:

> And as Peter was below in the courtyard, one of the maids of the high Priest came; and seeing Peter warming himself, she looked at him, and said, "You also were with the Nazarene, Jesus." But he denied it, saying "I neither know nor understand what you mean." And he went out into the gateway. And the maid saw him, and began again to say to the bystanders, "This man is one of them." But again he denied it. And after a little while again the bystanders said to Peter, "Certainly you are one of them; for you are a Galilean." But he began to invoke a curse on himself and to swear, "I do not know this man of whom you speak." And immediately the cock crowed a second time. And Peter remembered how Jesus had said to him, "Before the cock crows twice, you will deny me three times." And he broke down and wept. (14:66–72)

Luke tells us that as the cock crowed the second time:

> The Lord turned and looked at Peter. And Peter remembered the word of the Lord, how he had said to him, "Before the cock crows today, you will deny me three times." And he went out and wept bitterly. (Luke 22:61–63)

The awful thing about that look was not any accusation and reproach, but the anguish, the pity and the terrible grieving love it contained. Jesus knew the pain that burned through Peter. There is no pain like the pain of shame and self-loathing that comes upon us when we've trampled upon our best idea of ourselves, when we've been unfaithful to our friends, lovers, ideals; and waves of guilt and remorse sweep over us, sometimes driving us to despair, to thoughts of self-destruction. Jesus knew all this, because he knew the human heart. His look contained all the love God has for us as we destroy our own peace, and that is what made Peter break down and weep, not only from remorse, which is a kind of self-disgust, but out of repentance, which is an acute, radical recognition of our own situation, our own hopelessness, our own absolute need for the love of this God who seeks not to manipulate but to draw us by cords of love. And so the story in Part Two goes on to its devastating climax in the God-and-man-forsaken death of Jesus Christ.

The third part is a mysterious little epilogue in chapter 16, filled with impotence, weakness and fear. The ending is downbeat and inconclusive. Mark's Gospel probably ends at verse 8 of chapter 16, with a strange anti-climax. Some of the women who followed Jesus go to his tomb on the day after the Sabbath and find it empty, except for a mysterious young man who tells them Jesus has risen. They run away in distress and the book ends with the words: "for they were afraid".

Austin Farrer summed up this, probably the first Gospel to be written, in three lines, a line to each section:

> God gives you everything.
> Give everything to God.
> You can't.[1]

I realized, as I drove through the Scottish countryside, that this was *my* story. First of all, *I* need consolation and forgiveness. I need to know that I am accepted in spite of all I know against myself, in spite of my feebleness and compromises. Life is not straightforward, and being a good human being is not easy. In strange ways we constantly trip ourselves up and we are often ambushed by difficulties we never anticipated, hijacked by forces in our past and in our personality that we did not anticipate when we boldly committed ourselves to some great ideal or vision. Yet we long to be understood and accepted, even though we know so much against ourselves. And this is what we find in the first part of Mark's Gospel: healing, consolation, and the great pity of Christ.

But that is not enough. Something in us wants to go beyond the necessary given condition of our nature and personality. We do not want to use our private history and difficulties as an alibi for failure for ever, as a reason for acquiescing in weakness. Something in us still wants to be great and holy and heroic. We want to be able to give and not simply receive: if necessary we want to be able to give our life. We do not want always to be cowards clinging to our little security blankets; something in us wants to follow the lonely Christ in the high and austere way. So the great challenge of the second part of Mark's Gospel appeals to our idealism; and yet we know, after many false starts, how impossible it is. In an old phrase, we cannot pull ourselves off the ground by our own bootstraps.

Mark's pre-occupation with failure is very familiar to me. "God gives you everything. Give everything to God. You can't." We need to keep the three lines together. A religion of consolation alone is immature; it's baby food, Gerber spirituality, with no fibre, no challenge to it; spiritual mush, escapism. But a religion for heroes only can be a harsh and horrid thing, especially if it is successful. It can breed people who have lost touch with frail humanity, and who judge others from the cruel height of their own self-control. The strain begot by the constant struggle of self-denial often makes them haters of their own flesh. A religion for heroes can be a great and terrible trap. Awful things have been done by Christian heroes. We need the softening element of failure in our spirituality. We need to own our failure as disciples, we need to be radically honest, yet we must not succumb to despair. The hunger for holiness has to be kept alive in us. How do we move out of the impasse? How do we preserve a proper realism about ourselves, and yet continue to rise to the great supernatural challenge of Christ?

To answer that let us go back to John Mark himself, back to Mark the failure. Why did he write his book? To wallow in failure? Was his book an exercise in personal humiliation, or self-flagellation, the pitiless exposure of dreams that failed, of heroes who turned and fled? Well, not exactly. Mark wants us never to forget our failures and infidelities, but he told his story to point *beyond* human failure, to another possibility. Austin Farrer reminds us that there is, after all, a fourth line, and though it is only hinted at in Mark's little epilogue it is spelt out in the subsequent history of the church established by the deserters of Good Friday:

God Gives you everything.
Give everything to God.
You can't.
But Christ will make you able, for he has risen from the dead.[2]

The mystery that lies at the heart of Christian experience and rescues it from human despair is the mystery of the Resurrection of Christ from the dead. The disciples were clearly unprepared for it, as we are always unprepared for divine surprises. Something in us conspires with defeat and failure. Something in us is in love with death. Something in us hates the vision of the new and high and impossible dream. Mark knows we are afraid: afraid of our own failure; even afraid of divine possibility and its risks and discomforts. Mark wrote as he did, still scarcely believing *what* he wrote, because he and his friends had come to the end of human possibility and were surprised by the living possibility of God that met them on the other side of regret. They found, at last, a power, but not a power in themselves: at last they learned not to trust themselves, but to trust him. As self-admitted failures, they learned to trust the one who creates from nothing, and who brings life from death. Almost against their will, almost against their own patent disbelief, they discovered a new thing in their lives: they discovered grace beyond regret, and hope beyond fear. They discovered the Resurrection.

As we turn now and think about the Resurrection of Jesus Christ from the dead, the mysterious event that transformed the disciples, we have to remember a basic ambiguity in all the claims that faith makes about historical events. The encounter with the mystery of God always comes through some aspect of the universe we inhabit. Our own private experiences of the mystery of God are all located in time and space, because that is where *we* are located: they happen in dark corners of actual churches; on real mountain tops; during the reading of scriptures that are written in ink on paper; or as we are bathed in music made by the tapping of fingers on ivory or the drawing of horsehair along catgut. The divine disclosure is always mediated in particular events. There is no other way we can receive it, being what we are. If the divine mystery exists, then it must encounter us in this way; it must, in some sense, become flesh, become fact, become actual event. But the event, the fact, always remains ambiguous. It always has to be interpreted by faith. Argument is very little use here, because we cannot really argue from an account of the outward events themselves, such as a description of a range of hills, or the instruments of an orchestra, or the limestone wash on the walls of the church that revealed the hidden glory, and expect the description to work as argument or explanation. Only the heart and mind disposed to receive the revelation can know it through these events. Nor can an analysis of the means whereby the revelation was carried to the believer be used to negate the experience. People with ears to hear really hear music, though they know it is only created by the noise of hair rubbed against gut.

Jesus himself is the supreme example of this law. To those with eyes to see and ears to hear, he is the revelation of God, the embodiment of the divine mystery. To those who do not see or cannot hear, he is, as he was to many of the people of his time, only Joseph's son, whose relatives we know – and an unimpressive lot they are. Again, we are engaged in the inevitable circularity of all religious experience. Again, we have to affirm the fact that the meaning of spiritual or religious experience is found inside and not outside; its meaning is within and can only be understood after it is submitted to. The law of faith is defiantly unbudging in its paradoxical nature: in order to understand we must first believe. And this law applies, supremely, to the mystery of the Resurrection of Christ from the dead. We have to approach the Resurrection on two levels: there is, first of all, the level of the historical facts, the events that mediated the mystery itself; but we must also remember that there is an abiding distinction between the mystery mediated and the events that mediate it, although there is also an abiding and immovable connection between them. The mystery of the Resurrection was mediated to humanity through historical events, but an analysis of the events alone will not guarantee an encounter with the living Christ who is the meaning of the Resurrection. Nevertheless, Christianity as a historical religion, a religion that claims God has mediated himself through history, has a duty to give an account of the facts as it has received them. All we are called upon to do is to give an account of the hope that is in us, to set forth the times and the places of the events through which the mystery was mediated; if our listeners make the connection, it is because their outward sense has been befriended by faith and the revelation has been made.

Let us turn to the facts as we find them in the New Testament and try to understand what the claim is before we seek to understand its meaning. It is important to recognize that the event is described in a series of inconsistent accounts that contradict each other in matters of detail, though the central claim is consistent throughout. In a paradoxical way, this lends credence to the story; it is what we would expect from a variety of witnesses. We would get a series of contradictions, very often in a specifically detailed way, though we would expect the central event remembered to have a certain consistency in people's memories. In an earlier chapter I told the story of the Russian professor who invited a thug into his lecture to stage an event, which he then asked his students to describe. Inevitably, he received a number of different accounts of the event, though all agreed that some kind of violent uproar had ensued. The inconsistencies in the New Testament accounts suggest that there has been no orchestration, no cooking of the books, and this naivety serves to strengthen our trust in the writer's sincerity.

There seem to be five elements in the Resurrection claim: each element may be weak in itself, but cumulatively they are impressive. First is the fact that Jesus truly died on the cross. Crucifixion was usually a slow death. According to modern investigators, its victims really died of suffocation. When the nails were hammered into the extremities of a crucified person, the body was laid out on the cross and the arms would be extended at a 90-degree angle. However, when the cross was hoisted into an upright position the victims arms, with the weight of the entire body dragging on them, would sag to approximately 65 degrees. In that position the muscles would start to contract violently, cramps would spread from the forearms and upper arms to the shoulders, before moving into the limbs and trunk; spasms would cause the fingers and toes to curl inwards in a state of tetany, stomach muscles would tighten to form a hollow beneath the distended rib cage, the lungs would fill with air but, because of the contraction of the expiratory muscles, they would be unable to expel it and asphyxiation would set in. The only way to stave off death would be to relieve the drag on the hands and arms by using the nail through the feet as a fulcrum, enabling the victim to rise to an upright position. This manoeuvre would relax the effects of tetanization in the muscles and unload the air trapped in the lungs, but the effort would have been agonizing. The struggle for air would continue until exhaustion prevented the victim from raising himself upright and asphyxiation would then follow. If the victims lingered on, the soldiers hastened death by breaking the bones in their legs, thereby preventing them from pushing up for air. According to John's Gospel the two men who were crucified with Jesus had their legs broken in this way to hasten their asphyxiation. But when they came to Jesus they found that he was dead already, though one soldier, in order to leave an official stamp of death upon him, thrust a spear into his side.

The second element in the claim is that when the women came to the tomb on the day after the Sabbath they found it empty. All the Gospels agree with this fact, and so did the opponents of the Christian movement, because the story was spread around that the followers of Jesus had stolen his body. No one seems to have disputed the fact of the empty tomb itself. That, anyway, proves nothing. Controversy raged over *how* the tomb came to be empty. The followers of Jesus, after the initial fear, bewilderment and confusion, were persuaded that he had risen from the dead, but no magistrate would accept a story like that, so it was concluded circumstantially that his body had been stolen. No one seems to have challenged the central claim that the body was missing.

As I have said, an empty grave proves nothing, but the consistency of the claim has impressed some historians who are not believers, including Geza Vermes, the distinguished Jewish scholar. He clearly does not believe in what Christians mean by the Resurrection, but his analysis of the accounts leads him to conclude that the grave was probably empty when the followers of Jesus got there on the first day of the week.

The third element in the tradition is the series of appearances that are described variously in the Gospels, though the first and earliest account we have of them comes in Paul's first letter to the Corinthians, probably written about twenty years after the event. Paul's account is strong evidence:

> For I delivered to you as of first importance what I also received, that Christ died for our sins in accordance with the scriptures, that he was buried, that he was raised on the third day in accordance with the scriptures, and that he appeared to Cephas, then to the twelve. Then he appeared to more than five hundred brethren at one time, most of whom are still alive, though some have fallen asleep. Then he appeared to James, then to all the apostles. Last of all, as to one untimely born, he appeared also to me. (1 Corinthians 15:3–8)

It was the appearances themselves that gave meaning to the uninterpreted fact of the empty tomb. The empty tomb itself disclosed nothing. The meaning of the Resurrection was disclosed in the encounters, however we account for them, between Jesus and the disciples. Whether we call them mystical or spiritualistic experiences, they were, to the disciples, a strong and energizing proof that death had not cancelled the meaning and reality of Jesus Christ. They were emboldened by the experience to turn to the world and preach the idiocy of his Resurrection.

The fourth element is related to this, because it is difficult to believe that the kind of people Mark describes so mercilessly could have transformed themselves into nerveless and gifted confidence tricksters, stealing the body of Jesus in order to pretend he had been raised from the dead, especially when there was little to gain from the lie except derision and persecution. Paul sums up the argument perfectly:

> I protest, brethren, by my pride in you which I have in Christ Jesus our Lord, I die every day! What do I gain if, humanly speaking, I fought with beasts at Ephesus? If the dead are not raised, "Let us eat and drink, for tomorrow we die." (1 Corinthians 15:31–32)

The fifth element in this cumulative chain of evidence is the emergence of the Christian movement. The Gospels, as we have seen, are not sentimental about the disciples of Jesus. They show us on page after page that they did not understand Jesus. They had wanted a conventional messiah, a worldly leader, and Jesus had let them down. As one of them said a few days after his death, "We had hoped that he was the one to redeem Israel", but apparently he wasn't. He was yet another false messiah, another failure, and they all fell away. They all ran for cover in Gethsemane at the time of the arrest. Yet very soon they were confronting their own society with the extraordinary claim that this same Jesus who had been crucified was the one sent by God to bring people into a new way of living; and that he was not dead but alive and could be known now. An effect of that order of reversal and transformation must have a sufficient cause. When we see a large hole in a fence we know that something big must have crashed through it; in order to account for the extraordinary transformation of this unimaginative and ordinarily weak group of men into evangelists and martyrs, we must discover a sufficiently powerful cause. Their explanation for the change, and surely we must listen to it and give it credence, was the Resurrection. They located that transforming event on the first day of the week, and the very keeping of that day by the first Christians as a new sabbath is itself strong evidence. The first disciples were devout Jews, strongly committed to Jewish sabbath observance, yet soon they were keeping the next day, the *first* day of the week, as the *new* sabbath, the day of Resurrection.

The reverberations of that event in the garden where they laid him are still felt today. It is easy and fashionable to sneer at Christianity, its oddities and excesses, but much of the best in our heritage is linked to it and it continues to have a powerful effect on human history. A Swiss Reformer described the Church of God as an anvil that had worn out many hammers. And even if, because of its weakened state in secular Europe, we claim only to hear

> Its melancholy, long, withdrawing roar,
> Retreating to the breath
> Of the night-wind, down the vast edges drear
> And naked shingles of the world,[3]

it is provincial and insular of us to ignore its impressive strength in other parts of the world. That strength can not only be seen in numbers as in Africa and in North America, it is above all strong in the power to witness against tyranny and despair. We only have to think of the Church bravely witnessing against racism in South Africa; or the extraordinary Russian Church emerging strongly after generations of state-sponsored atheism; or the underground Church in China that has surfaced in recent years; or the

Church in South America in its solidarity with the oppressed; not to mention the countless quiet people who care for the poor and the outcast and go into the lost places of our society in love and with infectious gaiety. The Christian Church is indeed an anvil that has worn out many hammers and it will survive even in what John Betjeman called:

> Dear old, bloody old England
> Of telegraph poles and tin,
> Seemingly so indifferent
> And with so little soul to win.[4]

The Church will endure because its life is not based upon human strengths and certainties but upon the reality of God.

The experience of the disciples is best described as a transformation in hope. The Resurrection of Christ gave them an unconquerable new vision that ran against the tragic grain of history. The important thing for Christians today is not the establishment of the exact historical status of the Resurrection then, but the experience of the Resurrection now. Resurrection is the energy of unconquerable hope in life. It is not wishful thinking, it is hopeful acting. There is a kind of inertia in each of us and in human affairs in general: it is heavy and pessimistic and hopeless. Sometimes it is a general pessimism about the intractability or unimprovability of human affairs that sits upon us, fixing us to the spot, making it impossible for us to act or work for a better world: often it is a kind of private despair or fatalism over some habit we cannot shake off or some positive achievement that seems beyond our strength. The Resurrection summons us to a new energy of hope for our private lives as well as for human society; and history has shown what the principle of hope in life can do. Frightened and despairing people have discovered a grace in their lives that helped conquer despair and self-hatred. Even the intractable difficulties of politics are subject to hope. Societies can be improved, nation can learn to speak peace unto nation, and even churches can be renewed and feuding Christians reconciled. That is something of what we mean by believing in or experiencing the Resurrection now. The Easter Christ brought the disciples back from despair and released a new energy into history; not the obsessive energy that controls and overpowers, but the energy of hope that liberates and frees people for all sorts of new possibilities. The principle of Resurrection hope is revolutionary, because it releases us from the prison of the past, our institutional past as well as our private past. In our private lives it liberates us from the power of our own failures and the name of that liberation is forgiveness. Christ breaks the power of our own past if we will let him, if we will only resist the constant temptation to look back at the mistakes we made. One of the most extraordinary elements in Christian history is the way Christians have been able to reverse the past, not by rewriting it, but by robbing it of its power to control the future. Paul the murderer of Christians becomes the apostle to the Gentiles; Peter the deserter becomes the rock on which the Church is built; and so it has gone on down to our time. Paul captured the essence of this kind of hopeful looking to the future and away from the past and its failures in his letter to the Philippians:

Not that I have already obtained this or am already perfect; but I press on to make it my own, because Christ

Jesus has made me his own. Brethren, I do not consider that I have made it my own; but one thing I do, forgetting what lies behind and straining forward to what lies ahead, I press on toward the goal for the prize of the upward call of God in Christ Jesus. (Philippians 3:12–14)

But the principle applies to more than individuals and their private lives; it applies to societies and the great movements of history, and it applies to the Church itself. In all these institutions the principle of hope leads to action for positive change, for the creation of a juster society, as well as a purer and humbler Church. And again the record is impressive if we trace it in history. The abolition of the slave trade in the nineteenth century and the civil rights movement in this century were applications of the principle of Resurrection hope to apparently unalterable evils. The same is true of the improvement of living and working conditions for the poor in our own country. It is well known that the revolution in labour relations and rights of workers in Britain owed more to Methodism than to Marxism. And the struggle of hope goes on, in our society and throughout the world, the struggle to find another country where justice and peace dwell. And this is because, in Paul's language, "We look not to the things that are seen but to the things that are unseen", to the things that lie ahead, the things that wait for us, the perfecting of our nature, once forgiven, now to be transformed into the holiness God has in store for us; and the perfection of the peoples of the earth, so that the ugliness of cruelty and poverty will no longer disfigure the world. It is an amazing vision that calls to the best in each of us. Human history has not known a more generous or compelling one. It is an ideal to give our life to, a hope that gives life to our ideals. It is the call to seek another country and to serve another king.

One of the great themes of the New Testament is that of Christ as the pioneer, the one who goes ahead of us to prepare a way and a place for us. He always goes before us, into our future, into death itself, always looking back at us to draw us on in hope. There is no need now to be afraid, to stand rooted to the spot: he has gone on ahead and calls us forward. The messenger the women found at the empty tomb in Mark's Gospel told them that Jesus had gone before them into Galilee and they were to look for him there; and so must we. We have been freed from the past and are no longer its prisoners. We are to look for him in Galilee, in what lies ahead, in the long trail of our future.

PART II

5

SPIRIT

I will pray the Father and he will give
you another comforter. (John 14:16)

We rarely hear nowadays of children catching scarlet fever
or diphtheria, but they were serious scourges in Scotland
when I was a child. When I was ten I went down with scarlet
fever and had to be taken to hospital. The awful thing about
that particular disease was that you had to be isolated, and
were not allowed visitors. They did not have then today's
little glass cubicles that enable isolation patients to be visited
without risking infection through physical contact. I was
taken to a hospital five miles from my home and kept in
a big ward full of children. My family used to come and
stand on the path outside the ward and wave to me through
the window; that was as close as they were allowed. It was
kept there for six sad and homesick weeks. I have always
been prone to homesickness, and the six weeks were an
ordeal. I could never decide whether seeing my parents
outside on the path and being unable to talk to them and
touch them was worse than not seeing them at all. It was
good to know that they were still there and still loved me
enough to stand outside on many a cold afternoon, but it
was a terrible frustration just the same.

I think of that episode in my life when I meditate on the
fourteenth chapter in St John's Gospel, because it, too, is

suffused with sadness and frustration. Chapter 14 is part of what is called the final discourse by our Lord at the Last Supper. Immediately before chapter 14 opens, our Lord has told his disciples that he is soon to be taken from them: "Little children, yet a little while I am with you. You will seek me; and as I said to the Jews so now I say to you, Where I am going you cannot come" (13:33). They are already filled with that sense of foreboding and strange panic which makes us feel hollow and empty inside; the feeling we associate with airports and railway stations and all those partings that characterize our transient lives. That is bad enough, and casts a sombre cloud over the Last Supper, but worse is to come. Peter asks Jesus where is he going, and Jesus replies, "Where I am going you cannot follow me now; but you shall follow afterwards" (13:36). Characteristically, Peter promises to lay down his life for him, not knowing at that moment what Jesus is talking about: "Peter said to him, 'Lord, why cannot I follow you now? I will lay down my life for you' " (13:37). Then he is stunned by our Lord's prophecy that he would, that very night, deny him: "Jesus answered, 'Will you lay down your life for me? Truly, truly, I say to you, the cock will not crow, till you have denied me three times.' " (13:38). Peter never says another word during what is left of their time together. We can feel his stunned, almost sullen silence as he broods through the rest of the meal.

Sadness and confusion must have engulfed all eleven of his apostles, Judas having already gone out into the night. Jesus, loving them, as we are told, "unto the end", looks round at them and speaks words that have comforted millions as they gazed into the hopelessness of loss, and felt the unconsolable sorrow of death: "Let not you hearts be troubled . . . I go to prepare a place for you . . . I will come again and will take you to myself, that where I am you may be also. And you know the way where I am going." (14:1ff). Then Thomas, who liked everything clear and down to earth, speaks: "Lord we don't even know where you are going, so how can we know the way?" (14:5). Our Lord does not reply directly. Instead, he makes use of something that had happened the day before. Mark tells us in his fourteenth chapter that his disciples asked him where they were to keep the Passover. Jesus told them to go into the city and meet a man carrying a jar of water, who would lead them to the secret upper room already arranged, and there they were to make ready the Passover. They had not known where the room was or how to get there; the man had shown them the way (a man carrying a jar of water would be an unusual sight). In the same way, Jesus had come to show them the way to the Father. Not this time to a private upper room, where they might enjoy a few last hours together, made bittersweet by the great tearing apart they sensed coming upon them; but to that final home where there would be no parting, no separation, no helpless standing by as death claims its children. This time, they were going home to the Father and Jesus himself would guide them, be the true and living way to that permanent homecoming: "I am the way, and the truth, and the life; no one comes to the Father, but by me." It may seem to be a hard saying, but it was Jesus who taught us that God was our Father: not a judge to fear, or a potentate to be awed by, or an abstract principle that baffles us – but Father, the Father who is at home to us after all our wanderings.

Then Philip says the words that are often in our hearts. "Lord, show us the Father, and we shall be satisfied." There are so many ways in which that cry is our own. It reminds me, as I have said, of my own longing to see my parents when I was separated from them. We want some sign, however fleeting, that God loves us. We are not sure that he exists. We say with Job, "Oh, that I could find him!" If only he'd show us, just once, that he is there; reveal himself to us as he did to Moses and to those others who have seen him and been changed and for whom this world has lost its primary importance, for their eyes have seen the Lord, the God of hosts. Paul saw him, he tells us, and thereafter counted all the joys and beauty of this life as dross in comparison with the glory he had seen. Those of us who are filled with longing for God crave that vision: "Lord, show us the Father, and we shall be satisfied." In these chapters in John, our Lord is shown to have very little time left with his disciples who have not yet understood him. The words he spoke, the miracles that showed forth the glory of God, all have been misread or misunderstood. We can feel the edge of exasperation in his voice as he speaks to Philip: "Have I been with you so long and yet you do not know me, Philip? He who has seen me has seen the Father."

When I was in that hospital, I didn't want just to *see* my parents. I wanted to have them back totally and be taken into their arms. I wanted to be at home with them. Seeing was something, but it was not enough, it did not satisfy, because I was more than a pair of eyes, and it was all of me that wanted all of them. So it is in our longing for God: we won't be satisfied till we have God completely and utterly – everything else merely tantalizes. God knows this, knows our condition, and has stooped down to it. According to the author of John's Letters, in Christ we beheld God's glory, we touched the divine glory and spoke to it. That is the message of John's Gospel summed up in the opening words of the first letter of John:

> That which was from the beginning, which we have heard, which we have seen with our eyes, which we have looked upon and touched with our hands, concerning the word of life – the life was made manifest, and we saw it, and testify to it, and proclaim to you the eternal life which was with the Father and was made manifest to us – that which we have seen and heard we proclaim also to you . . . (1 John 1:1–3)

Indeed, the whole New Testament is the sworn testimony of those who saw these things and learned, so slowly, what they meant – and the memory of what they saw, heard and handled has been passed down through history by the Christian community. The God we long to see, once came among us. The glory was seen on earth. Has it now departed? Are we left only with a handful of ancient testimonies, the fading memory of a once vivid experience? Is that glory something seen, if it is seen at all, only from afar, or is it something that may be known now, experienced today? Can we get closer to God than I got to my parents during those six sad weeks I was in Hospital?

The answer Christians give to those questions is the answer Jesus gave to his anxious disciples on the night before he died. There would be a way in which Christ, taken from them in crucifixion and restored for a season to them in the Resurrection, would be with them always. Christians call this experience the Holy Spirit. They talk about the "inward testimony of the Holy Spirit", and by that strange phrase they are trying to describe the experience of an interior process of assent that helps them bridge the gap between time past and time present, between language about God and the experience of God. Language about God, especially the language of Christian memory we call scripture, by itself can communicate nothing to us; it does not make sense to us until we learn to pay attention to that invisible reality within us. It is this inward prompting or testimony, this interior sense of correspondence between what is heard with our ears and understood with our heart, that persuades or converts us. It is this inward assent that enables us to translate the external evidence into conviction. Without it the evidence, though it may be perfectly valid in itself, will not persuade. There seems to be some parallel between this interior disposition towards faith and certain types of creative activity among men and women.

What is creativity? What is happening in the creation of a poem or the composing of a piece of music? Some poets and musicians would say it is a matter of capturing and putting down on paper something that comes to them. Sir Edward Elgar said that music was in the air and that you simply took as much of it as you wanted. And poets talk about their poems coming to them. There seem to be latent in reality whole universes of meaning that the creative artist apprehends and sets down for the rest of us. Artists clothe the meanings they perceive in forms we can apprehend. Each genuine poem is an incarnation of grace and truth. And while it is true that most of us lack the genius to discover and re-create the poem, we have enough of it in us to enable us to recognize it when it is set down.

There is a similarity between the mysterious processes of artistic creativity and the processes of the spiritual life. At the very least, we can say that the creation of art and its recognition by those of us who are not artists is an analogy of the life of faith. The thing created, be it in word or music, does not come at first with an explanatory leaflet*. It comes as it is, bearing its own life, but something in us recognizes it, understands it in a way that is deeper than immediate discourse about it. It is only after we acknowledge it in this way, believe in it, that we are able to understand it or attempt to explain it. The faith in the thing, our recognition of it, always precedes our understanding of it, the mere ability to explain it. There is always a quality of revelatory surprise in true art, which is why it frequently outstrips our ability to comprehend it. Evelyn Underhill talked of "the huge disparity between the unspeakable experience and the language that will most nearly suggest it". The artist, like the mystic in seeking to share a vision, must bewitch her audience, catch them up to something of her state, before they can be made to understand. And the artistic dialogue continues because we have some capacity for entering into the consciousness of the artist; we can be caught up into something of the artist's state.

We must be careful not to make an absolute distinction between the life of faith and the life of art. Both, in some sense, connect us with transcendence, with the reality that encompasses us, but from which we are mysteriously estranged. There has been a remarkable contraction of religious consciousness in secular European culture throughout this century, so much so that art has become the only acceptable and available medium through which

---

* Inevitably, of course, explanations and interpretations are offered and begin the process of the creation of secondary sources which soon almost obliterate the primary experience, giving rise to the parasitic disciplines of criticism, one of which is theology.

many men and women can transcend themselves. The irony is that it is poetry and music that seem to be keeping the vocabulary of religion alive, even if the experience behind the vocabulary is dead.

On way of accounting for this situation is by affirming the reality of a dynamic principle of continuity between ourselves and the transcendent reality that haunts us and from which comes a whole range of experiences, stretching from mystic consciousness to the crafting of a sonnet. Christians call that principle of continuity, Holy Spirit. We have no monopoly in it, but we give it a specific reference and identity. And the language used to describe the experience of the Spirit has a twofold resonance: it is something that dwells in us, if only as a latency, a potentiality; but it is also something that transcends us, something that dwells with God. Classical language about God has always stressed this duality: God is transcendent and immanent, he is at the same time far from us, yet close to us, within us. Prayer is our reaching out in longing to the God who, in Hopkins' language, "lives, alas, away"; yet Paul tells us that it is the Spirit that prays within us. It is this indwelling reality which is the source of our longing for God and our struggle to be good.

The word "spirit" itself offers us a clue to the meaning of the reality we are seeking to understand, even if we are wary of exactly defying it. Anyone who has ever seen a dead body will understand the force of the word "spirit". Long ago people looked at the living and at the dead and they wondered at the change that death brought to men and women. What was it that changed this vigorous, laughing child into a motionless statue? The obvious thing that struck them was that the dead person did not breathe, there was no movement in the chest. To be dead meant to have no breath, and to be alive, to have power to rise up and run and shout, meant to have breath. Not surprisingly, they concluded that this breath was the very principle of life. This is why in so many languages the word for breath comes to mean not only the air that fills the lungs, but the mystery and power of life itself that fills the living being. In Latin this word is *spiritus*, from which our word "spirit" comes. Each of us has this spirit. It is not just something we draw into our lungs. It is much more than that. Spirit is the very force, the very power of life. In death the spirit goes out of us, leaving us an empty husk. We cannot see the human spirit, but at death we can recognize its absence. Human spirit is what makes us alive, not dead. It is the power of life within us. Holy Spirit is a vaster reality than human spirit, though there is continuity between them. If the human spirit fills a single individual, Holy Spirit is the principle of life that fills the universe, it is the life that activates the whole creation.

The book of Genesis tells us that it was this Spirit that moved upon the face of the waters, breathing the principle of life into them, creating the conditions that would give rise to the whole chain of being. But Holy Spirit in the Old Testament is more than a trigger for life, a latent capacity for evolution implanted in creation. It is the Spirit that generates the complex we call human culture by inspiring men and women to become creators. The implication is that the human creature has been created a spiritual being that is self-conscious and able to participate in the continuing adventure of creation. It is our spiritual capacity, the principle of continuity between human spirit and Holy Spirit that enables us to be discoverers, creators, and not just adapters who automatically conform to the laws that govern their being. This is the capacity that enables us to respond to revelation, the disclosing of meaning from the mysterious reality that encompasses us. There is always a difficulty here, and the process seems to be highly selective, but there have always been creatures of peculiar genius who see further and recognize more than the rest of us, and we are able to participate by proxy in their discoveries, not because their language or other medium of expression is able perfectly to capture what has been revealed to them, but because there is enough spiritual capacity in us to comprehend it. We could say that we have a capacity for revelation, a capacity for the Spirit, we are *capax Dei*, capable of God and the marvellous richness of his being.

Holy Spirit is not the possession of the Church, not a commodity in which it has exclusive rights. It is the divine life, penetrating all of creation, informing and provoking human genius; the source of inspiration, from whose energy is derived the holiness of the saint and the vision of the artist. It is for this reason that God will never be without witnesses and it is for this reason that the most effective testimony to the power of Spirit is not infrequently found outside what is called organized religion. It is entirely possible that in an age which is witnessing the gradual, even if only partial collapse of religious consciousness, it will fall to the poet, the musician and the painter to be the channels of the Spirit, the agents through which consciousness of transcendence is maintained. That may appear to be a bleak prospect; in fact it is a cheering one. If the Holy Spirit is the divine energy that fills all things, then it will find modes of expression everywhere, long after its official protectors have ceased to convince. On the other hand, it is this very fact that is the

Church's best hope, because it finds creation in some sense prepared for its message. The folly of the Church's proclamation, like the madness of true art, is responded to be the presence of the Spirit within us. It may indeed be the case that the world has ceased to respond to the Church because the Church has ceased to respond to the Spirit, and it is only as the Spirit's agent that it can win a hearing.

The recognition that "the Spirit has filled the world", the conviction that it is a universal reality, is fundamental, but it is not, for Christians, the only experience of the Spirit. As we have seen, the centre of Christian experience lies in the Incarnation, the doctrine that the Divine Nature revealed itself in the man Jesus, the Word became flesh. The real scandal of Christianity lies in this quite specific historical claim. Christians claim that certain events of two thousand years ago were a concentrated focus of revelation, very much as a chink of light in a well-shuttered room can throw a beam of illumination into the farthest corner. But powerful as this claim is, it is still an image of distance and separation for us. We are here in the midst of time and its confusions and God's revelation in Christ was in another place, at another time. It is here that Christians claim a quite specific experience of Holy Spirit; and the evidence for that claim is experimental or experiential; it is an invitation to test the claim by life rather than by logic.

There is an important sentence in John's Gospel: "I will pray the Father, and he will give you another Counsellor, to be with you for ever" (14:16). As we have already noticed, Christ, when he said these words, was leaving the disciples, but he promised them something in his stead, "another Counsellor". The word the RSV translates as "counsellor" is really untranslatable into English. In Greek it is *parakletos*.

The AV translates it "comforter", other versions say "advocate", "helper", "strengthener" and some just give up and transliterate it into "Paraclete". It comes from a verb that means to call to one's side for support, guidance and strengthening. It is something we have probably done ourselves or responded to when done by another: some great crisis or tragedy is upon us and we pick up the telephone and get our best friend on the line: 'Something has happened. I need you, come over immediately." In Greek the verb for that call for help would be *parakaleo*, and the person who responded with immediate care would be a *parakletos*. In fact, all the ways of translating this word contain an important truth.

Christ was a comforter and the one he left in his stead is a comforter, and the evidence for this claim is experiential. A Christian is facing death or is in great weakness or trouble and seeks the ministry of the Church, either through the laying-on of hands or by anointing. The priest prays for the Holy Spirit the Comforter to be with that person, and that is what happens: through the sacrament, through the love and concern of the Church, comfort comes, calmness steals over the person who experiences the reality of scripture's claim that "underneath are the everlasting arms". Of course, this is not only expressed or ministered exclusively through the clergy: the Comforter works through all of us. One of the ways we express the presence of the Comforter is by holding one another, by trying to pour our love and strength into someone else who is troubled. What is being experienced here is an actualizing, a representing of Christ through the dynamic reality of the Holy Spirit. This experience is at the heart of the sacramental life of the Church. The mystery of the sacraments is very like the mystery of creation with which the artist struggles. To the eye of the ordinary, uninterested beholder nothing unusual is going on, but to the eye of faith, the visionary eye, there is set up a ladder to heaven.

Christ continues to mediate his comfort through the experienced reality of the Holy Spirit. There is much comfort in Christian faith still, but a religion of comfort only is a distorted religion, we might call it hot-water-bottle Christianity. There *is* much comfort but there is something else as well, and the clue lies in the other meaning that can be given to comfort. The Paraclete comes not only to console us but to disturb us, provoke us, prod us forward. A religion without the element of disturbance, a smooth and comforting religion that never challenges us or provokes us to self-denial and heroic effort, is a pathological religion, a childish religion. Christianity is full of comfortable works spoken to us by our Saviour, but it is also full of uncomfortable words, words spoken by Christ to challenge our weakness and selfishness, words that provoke our prejudices and breach our defences. And that provocative task is still fulfilled in the Church through the goading energy of the Holy Spirit, the one sent to provoke us by the words and lives of the uncomfortable ones who call us to holiness and heroism. Christ comes to us not only through the grace of the sacraments but through the spirit of prophecy, by means of the passionate infilling of the few who are sent to disturb the many. And that is as much a fact of Christian experience, as much an experience of the Holy Spirit, as is the grace and comfort that are also signs of his presence.

The *Parakletos* is also our guide and teacher. Christian truth is dynamic, it is vast and paradoxical, and one of the functions of the Paraclete is to guide is into all truth, to confront us with truths we may have ignored or found uncongenial. The Faith might have been "once and for all delivered to the saints", but we must always seek new ways of interpreting it to the men and women of our time, and we must be sensitive to the new unfoldings of truth prepared for our generation and perhaps heard by no other. The Church has, in fact, experienced and continues to experience this probing guidance from the Holy Spirit. Another way of describing this phenomenon is by talking about the development of Christian belief. Christians claim that their teachings are rooted in scripture, but any student of theological history knows that the incidents or principles rooted in scripture have been developed and elaborated into quite complex ideas that are far from explicit in the Bible. Our claim is that these are not new inventions but developments of implicit truths which we recognized under the guidance of the Holy Spirit.

Christian doctrine is more like a river than a reservoir and it powers its way unpredictably through history. And this image of a powerful river suggests the final aspect of the activity of the Holy Spirit, the Paraclete. It is often depicted as a sort of raw energy or power, like wind or fire that can sweep through people and fill them with abilities and strengths they never dreamed they possessed. One of the most pronounced aspects of Christ was his power. We feel the strength and conviction that were in him pouring off the pages of the New Testament. We feel his energy, his potency rising to meet us, stalking behind us. And one of the most extraordinary promises of Christ was that, with the power of the Paraclete given to us, we would do even greater things than Christ: "Truly, truly, I say to you, he who believes in me will also do the works that I do; and greater works than these will he do, because I go to the Father" (John 14:12). This promise brings us face to face with one of the most controversial elements in Christian history. To what extent can Christians today expect the type of supernatural activity recorded in the New Testament, described as done in the power of the Spirit? For centuries the signs and wonders recorded in the New Testament were thought of as unique and unrepeatable. The technical name for this point of view is 'dispensationalism': the miracles reported in the New Testament were part of the unique activity of Jesus and the early Church. But that period came to an end and we are no longer to expect such supernatural interference. Nervousness about unpredictable outbursts of spiritual power among members of the Church has always characterized Church leaders, who jealously guard institutional Christianity from the excesses of unlicensed zealots. But the desire of leaders to control the Church is not the only reason behind suspicion of spectacular spiritual activity. A rejection of the supernatural claims of the New Testament has been one of the basic assumptions of much recent scholarly comment on scripture. If we assume that miracles do not occur, then we have to find natural explanations for those that are described in the New Testament. The combination of the modern rejection of what the New Testament calls "signs and wonders" and the nervous desire of Church leaders to confine them to the Church's infancy has removed supernatural expectations from Christian consciousness. Any debate about signs and wonders is confined to the status of events in the New Testament.

The new and explosive element in the situation is what is called the neo-Pentecostal movement that has erupted in twentieth-century Christianity and is now strongly rooted in most Churches, including the Catholic Church. What characterizes this movement is the claim that the supernatural activity recorded in the New Testament is still being experienced. Neo-Pentecostalists or charismatics, unlike many Christians in the traditional Churches, have a high level of expectation of direct divine activity in their lives. They believe that the promises of Jesus in the New Testament that his disciples would do his works, and even greater works, in his name are valid today. They claim that healings, signs and wonders still occur. They claim that conventional Christianity has allowed itself to be hypnotized by the fearful and the faithless, while to those with faith all things are still possible.

There have been excesses and rigidities associated with this movement, but it has radically transformed Christianity in the twentieth century and re-introduced the elements of surprise and expectation in Christian experience. And it has powerfully illustrated the strength and unpredictability of the Spirit that continues to "blow where it lists".

So the Paraclete is comforter, disturber, teacher and guide, energizer; in fact, everything Jesus was to his disciples the Paraclete is supposed to be to us. Jesus Christ comforted and disturbed, he taught and empowered his disciples, and the results are the wonder of history. A handful of ordinary men and women burst upon the world and transformed it. They did greater works than Christ did: they created a Church that has comforted millions down the ages, a Church that has disturbed the easy conscience of humanity, a Church that has taught the nations and was, for centuries, the protector of learning and guardian of culture, a Church that empowered men and women with strength to change their ways, to turn around and walk away from self-destruction and darkness into the abundant life of fulfilled humanity. And all this has been done through the Paraclete, "the other Comforter", the Holy Spirit sent into the Church by Christ to be the manner of his abiding presence until his return in glory.

But the important truth for Christians and the reality for all men and women, whether or not they acknowledge it, is the great fact celebrated in the book of Wisdom that "the Spirit of the Lord hath filled the whole world", and continues to infuse and penetrate all human culture and every good deed. That is why God is never left without witnesses and why the church, at the moment in one of its distraction fits, should not fret. All will be well,

Because the Holy Ghost over the bent
World broods with warm breast and with ah! bright
    wings.[1]

6

CHURCH

You are fellow citizens with the saints
and members of the household of God.
(Ephesians 2:19)

Professional Christians, Church leaders or preachers, become
terribly aware that they are walking contradictions, licensed
frauds. On the one hand, as public figures we represent the
Christian message, and people project on to us their own
expectations and longings. To some extent we are vicarious
figures, there to be the person or *parson*, the one who
represents God and the spiritual life to those who are too
busy to spend much time on it themselves; we become the
persons whose job it is to keep the rumour of God alive in
history. And yet we know that we are, in fact, not anything
like the stained glass window that some people imagine us
to be, want us to be or think we ought to be. Inside we are
just as full of doubts, fears, anxieties, lusts, longings, as
everyone else. This realization tends to creep up on us as
we get into middle age and become more aware of our own
frailty and fallibility. When we are young we are still trying
on different characters for size, testing different ideals; and
it is very easy to assume that because we admire an ideal
and think we ought to conform to it, that we are able to.
It is only as we move further into time that we realize that
many of the things we most admire are beyond us and that

we are not at all like the heroes we thought we could easily imitate in our youth. This accounts for the flatness, jadedness, even cynicism or bitterness that sometimes characterizes middle-aged clergy. They have come to realize how difficult it is to be spiritually and morally heroic, and how wide a gap there is between their own tepid spirituality and the reality of God and the expectations of their people. Hence the sense of fraudulence. If we are aware of the gap we sometimes feel like telling people, "No, you've got it wrong. I'm not like that. I'm actually a very messed-up human being." But, of course, to do that would probably be self-indulgent and even if we attempted it people would be likely to say, "Isn't he modest? Isn't he human, just like the rest of us?", and treat even our confession as evidence that we are special. In a funny kind of way it is both a 'no win' and 'no lose' situation. We are here in the middle of all this confusion, knowing how inappropriate we are as vessels of God's disclosure and yet also knowing that in all sorts of ways that is precisely what we are. God *does use* these frauds, these very flawed and confused creatures, to address, comfort, challenge, console people. Back we come again to the ambiguity, the ambivalence. We are still very much flesh, blood and galloping neuroses, yet through all that God reaches people.

If we leave ministers and move into the church buildings they serve, we find the same two-sidedness, the same ambiguity. There are a number of buildings I know and like, churches, holy places, which are very important to me. It is very difficult to define what it is about these places that draws me. They are obviously material structures built by human hands – stone and oak, brass, paintwork – and yet some of these buildings speak overwhelmingly of holiness, of otherness; in the language used by the spiritualists, they are 'thin' places, transparent places. The sense of the other world, the other place we long for, seems palpable, almost within touching distance. I find buildings of this sort aching and tantalizing, almost painful in their sweetness and power. I sit in them and I am often close to tears, because they communicate a sense of presence and a sense of absence at the same time; they fill me with a longing for that which I do not yet possess. And this poignancy, this sort of aching and longing that is both fulfilled and frustrated as we visit holy buildings, can be heightened if there is a priest at the altar dressed, perhaps, in eucharistic vestments, reverently celebrating the sacrament, as I have done so many times myself down the years. Perhaps he appears to the onlooker to be a very ikon of Christ, a mediator of heavenly realities, and one receives the sacrament gladly from such holy hands. Yet behind the holiness, the quietness, the devout composure at the altar, there may be and almost certainly is, at least from time to time, a churning, confused human being who communicates to others what he does not always succeed in holding on to himself. He is one of T.S. Eliot's "wounded healers" who cannot heal himself. So we confront yet again the extraordinarily powerful ambiguity, where the holy, the other, the divine, is both contradicted, interrupted and yet is, nevertheless, expressed by the humanity in which it dwells, or through which it touches other human beings.

And when we think about it, how else could it be done? How else could the divine reach us, except through such secondary instruments, mediators, things that channel the divine to us? Whatever the divine is, it is never actually *in* but comes *through* these human or material instrumentalities, which is why they tantalize us and fill us with an aching longing, because they suggest more than they actually deliver. How else could it be? The divine uses what is available, both to it and to us. If the divine is to be made available to us, then it must come to us through the confusion of our senses, in people, in places, in snatches of music and glimpses of countryside, in sudden half-seen illuminations, in whispers heard under the rush and noise of life. The divine mystery clothes itself in creation, in all its heartbreaking muddle and beauty. This is what theologians mean by the sacramental principle. The transcendent, divine reality, the invisible mystery of God, is expressed or disclosed in outward and visible signs that convey something of the value of God to us, rather in the way money, with its paper and coins, conveys value to us, although a Bank of Scotland pound note, for example, is not itself a pound of gold.

This disclosure of the divine that comes in hints and symbols, in the ache and longing of beauty, both in people and in places, is for those with eyes to see, ears to hear and faith to interpret, fully expressed in the life of Jesus. It is the same principle in all its ambiguity that we have been observing, brought here to a clarity and fulfilment that is unique. And this claim obviously cannot be argued or demonstrated. The ambiguity endures, even here, in Jesus Christ: "Is not this the carpenter's son, whom we know, whose brothers and sisters we work beside and argue with, meet in the local tavern, do business with?" Indeed he is, he is all these things. And yet he is also the disclosure of God, for those whose minds and hearts are open to him. What we have in the New Testament is the record of a growing awareness among his followers that Jesus was more than a prophet or a particularly good man, but was, in a sense language could not adequately express, the very presence, the very fullness of the experience of God in a human life; what John Robinson called, "the human face of God", God at last fully and humanly expressing himself, but this time without the interruptions and the contradictions, the flaws and the fraudulence that all other means of conveying the divine inevitably involve. In this case, the human will was the perfect vehicle of the divine, because here was a human will that conformed itself utterly to the divine will. Here was a nature that didn't get in its own muddled way, but surrendered itself in absolute simplicity to the Father's will. Here was a nature that became the perfect vehicle for the divine mystery. What in our case interrupts, confuses and muddles the divine disclosure, was in his case the perfect transmitter, the unflawed window, the clear opening to the beyond, the perfect revelation. And flesh and blood cannot reveal this to us, nor any argument or build-up of logical symmetry. It comes, as we say, by *revelation*: it is an act of recognition, a kind of coming into a state of love and knowledge, where scales drop from our eyes and we know that this is he. "Who do men say that I am?" he asked the disciples, and heard from Peter the great confession: "You are the Christ, the one who bears the true likeness of God."

This is what the Church means by the Incarnation, the claim that the Eternal God who reaches out to us in hint and symbol, in our longings and losses, makes himself known to us, in these last days, in flesh, in the person of Jesus of Nazareth. This accounts for the Christian Church. The Church has been called "the extension of the Incarnation"; and there is some force in the description, though only if we remember that the Church obscures Christ and the mystery of God as much as it reveals them, whereas the ambiguity in Christ (that is to say, the possibility of misinterpreting Christ or failing to see the mystery of God at work in him) had more to do with the blindness and deafness of those who saw and heard him than with any intrinsic flaw in his nature. Nevertheless, there is an unavoidable risk involved in the very principle of Incarnation. Just as we can ignore signals from each other, tokens of love, signs of discomfort and unease; just as we can ignore and be inattentive to all that, because of its subtlety or because we are too brutally preoccupied to notice, so there is an avoidability about God's approach to us. Nevertheless, the Church can legitimately be called the extension of the Incarnation, inasmuch as it is the movement that flowed from that encounter between God and humanity, concentrated in the man Jesus of Nazareth. The Church extends in history from that point and continues to reflect upon, wrestle with and seek to be the vehicle of that divine – human encounter. It continues to be a means of the divine approach, the divine self-disclosure, an appointed place for engagement or meeting with God. But the same tantalizing logic of ambiguity pertains. The Church is 'yes' and 'no'; it discloses and obscures God; it is stone and oak, and though "stone and oak decay, give no stay", yet through the perishable the imperishable is glimpsed and mediated. "This also is thou; neither is this now", as Charles Williams put it.

As we sit in the middle of the stone and oak and limewash, and watch the flickering light of sanctuary lamp and candle, we encounter the divine. In spite of death-watch beetle and crumbling timbers, mischievous choristers and troubled

117

priests, divinity is still encountered. Again, this is the way it has to be according to our nature. We need our priests to be touched with our infirmities, our surgeons wounded, the hands that heal us to bleed with compassion, because we know that we, too, are far from perfect: indeed are made afraid and lonely by perfection. What we need is the homeliness and muddle that God uses to sting us into repentance and rededication. We don't want, and certainly will never get, a Church or Christian community that is without spot or wrinkle. There's a certain irony in Paul's language about the Church as the pure bride of Christ. In spite of the Church's white wedding dress, we know she has been around, we know she is not what she would like us to believe she is. She is like the tragic clown in Kierkegaard's parable who was sent into the town to tell the people that the big top was on fire and would they come and help to extinguish it, but the people laughed at such marvellous clowning and the circus was burned to the ground. The Church is the bearer of momentous tidings that are confused and muddled by her own reputation and obvious imperfections. It is small wonder the world doesn't always hear us, or laughs at us when it does, because we are indeed a strange and motley crew.

This same glorious ambiguity characterizes all aspects of the Church's life. Indeed, the Church itself is the best example of the ambiguity. Institutional Christianity is a baffling phenomenon to contemplate. The disunity of the Church is a proverbial target for pulpit rhetoric about our "unhappy divisions", but it provides us with the best illustration of the dilemma of historical Christianity. Christ preached and exemplified a very radical repudiation of the world and its use of power. Power, control and force are the ways in which assertive, greedy and unfulfilled people try to win a place for themselves in the struggle of life. The way of unpower, the way that unshackles and liberates people, is the way of God revealed by the Jesus who came among us as God's servant.

This freeing of people from their bondage to power, what theologians call redemption, was the work of Jesus. The movement that preserves what has been called "the dangerous memory" of Jesus can only have integrity if it seeks, however clumsily, to reflect that radical message of liberation in its own life and structures. Historically, the Christian movement has never fully obscured this message, though it has only intermittently proclaimed it in its own life and teaching. But almost in spite of itself the dangerous memory has been preserved, both in scripture and in the witness of inspired individuals. We have to admit, however, that from the earliest times the Church has denied the Gospel by its own will to control others and have power over them. We have already thought of the kind of power disputes we find in the New Testament between the disciples. They were the forerunners of generations of Christian leaders who have accommodated the memory of Jesus to the mind of the world. Since James and John, the sons of Zebedee, sought to sit at Jesus' side in his kingdom, their example has been followed by generations of disciples who have followed their lead and placed themselves in positions of prominence and authority in the Christian movement, usually in opposition to other aspiring leaders. Most of the disputes that divide Christians are still in the area disputed over by James and John. There is a sort of 'Zebedee syndrome' in the history of the evolution of Christian ministry. The big contenders in the dispute about ministry are papacy versus bishops versus presbyterian systems versus congregational forms of leadership versus various forms of charismatic leadership that have claimed their authorization directly from God rather than from any ecclesiastical authority. We could probably find something to affirm in each form of Church government, and a wise Church policy would probably combine elements from them all, but the point to notice here is that each can fall into the Zebedee trap of claiming exclusive authority for itself. Disputants in ecclesiastical politics always believe themselves to be exceptions to any standard set by Christ. They are only a special case of the normal human blindness and egocentricity that believes itself to have been miraculously preserved from the normal dynamics of human pride and folly. The mind of Christ seems to be clear enough on the subject of power disputes among his followers, yet they have been the most conspicuous characteristic of the history of institutional Christianity.

So Christian ministry, while it has undoubtedly been a source of blessing to the Church, has also been a deadly weight. The inescapable dilemma lies in our need for leadership, even though leaders set up a magnetic field that draws power towards themselves. The real dilemma that faces the Christian leader is the duty to lead but in as Christlike a way as possible. Christian leadership is self-emptied and must seek to protect the health of the whole Church and not the rights of the leadership group or system. It will always be an ambiguous necessity. It is the most controversial example of the dual nature of all the instruments that mediate something of the glory of God to us. This is the principle behind all the sacraments: these strange, homely, matter-of-fact things we do with bread, wine, water and words, that are yet also the coming of the divine, the mediating of grace. We can't better the old definition of the sacrament as an outward and visible sign of an inward and spiritual grace. The outward and visible both conveys grace and yet obscures grace. As it does with ministers and the buildings they serve, so it does with all the other coins in this exchange between the divine and the human.

There is, for instance, a sacrament of preaching. We have all from time to time been rendered nearly mad with boredom as we have sat under platitude piled upon platitude, or felt the anger or anxiety of the lonely person in the pulpit. Yet we have also been stung to the heart, quickened to tears, have caught a glimpse of the holiness and compassion of Christ through the folly of preaching. And those of us who do it have felt ourselves to be conduits of both sides of this monstrous paradox, bearers of Christ and killers of Christ; sometimes being found by the word, the single word that cleanses and consoles, and yet sometimes drowning ourselves and our hearers in word and more words. And the same is true of the other sacraments. We have taken the bread which is Christ's body, we have administered the wine of his new life, and we have known him in the breaking of the bread. And yet sometimes we have taken the sacrament without thought, sometimes we have obscured it by our own idiosyncrasy, or drawn attention to ourselves rather than to the one who comes among us in the breaking of the bread.

But there are graver offences to report. The Christian sacrament of the Eucharist has been fought over almost as much as the Christian doctrine of ministry. It is a melancholy fact that the sign of Christ's abiding presence in his Church has been the most potent symbol of Christian self-hatred.

As with the debate on the ministry, the trouble seems to be a problem of control, another 'Zebedee syndrome'. From the earliest times, access to the sacrament seems to have been heavily controlled by the leadership in local communities, showing how much difficulty the Church has experienced from the very beginning in responding to the insane mercy of the Christ who gives each of us the same wages, no matter how little or long we have laboured. Of course, holiness of life is one of the purposes for which the sacraments were given, but they were not given as official rewards for good behaviour. It is not easy to see how the fateful connection between sacrament and discipline could have been avoided, but it has served, at times, to turn the sacrament of the Christ who refused to follow the way of power into a mechanism of control. The most virulent example of this travesty was the use, usually for political reasons, of the instrument of excommunication by the medieval papacy. In the carefully articulated hierarchy of medieval society this usually had a devastating effect. No less devastating was the effect of Protestant discipline, especially for sexual sins, in puritan societies. The effect of using the Eucharist in this way is to separate it from the life of Jesus, the man who did not resist evil and refused the way of coercion in his ministry.

Related to the mechanism of morally protecting the sacrament from the abuse of sinners, is the practice of fencing it off against those who do not religiously qualify for it. This type of instrumentalizing of the sacrament is related to the attempt to turn Christian ministry into a power structure. This works in two ways. The theory of ordination may hold that a supernatural power is transmitted to the ordained person to create the sacrament by the use of the right words and gestures, accompanied by a right intention. The motive behind mechanistic theories of the sacrament like this is the proper one of guaranteeing the promise of Christ to the worshipper, but it achieves it by removing the sacrament from the human or relational sphere into a realm of false and almost automatic objectivity. The faithfulness of Christ's promise is replaced by a formal system that claims to authenticate the presence of Christ by a measurable and objective criteria. But if you know how to measure and guarantee a genuine Eucharist, you also know how to identify a false or invalid one. Again the powerless body of Christ is used as a theological weapon in quasi-political disputes among Christian.

And even Churches in the Protestant tradition that would claim to avoid such methods of eucharistic warfare, use the sacrament in their own way as an instrument of discrimination, most notably by their exclusion of children from its reception. They do not validate the efficacy of the sacrament by a list of objective criteria, but tend to fall into the trap of what is called *receptionism*, which places the onus on the recipient, either by stringent moral qualifications or by a rigorous intellectual grasp of the mystery of the sacrament, thereby excluding the young or mentally disadvantaged or disabled. All of these approaches to the sacrament of the Eucharist conform it more closely to human patterns of control than to the pattern of divine helplessness and self-emptying.

The other historic area of dispute that has turned the sacrament of the Eucharist into a battlefield is the nature of the change in the bread and wine. The passion for precision in meaning and understanding, itself a kind of control, has brought to the mystery of Christ's presence in the Eucharist a whole host of questions that are incapable of final answers and ought never to have been put. What is the exact change wrought in the bread and the wine? At what point does it occur? Who has the power to effect the change? Can that power ever be removed? The answers to these inappropriate questions have divided Christians for centuries, especially in the West, where there is less patience with mystery and uncertainty than in the mystical East. The eucharistic controversies serve to remind us that the intellect and understanding seek power and control, even over the mystery of God. This special case of the undying human urge to dominate and exercise authority over reality has particular poignancy in disputes about the status of the broken body of Christ. It is not the supreme example among the many paradoxes of Christian history, but it is a major one, nevertheless. It is a far greater scandal than the sum of all sinful communions, because it is a measured contradiction of the words and example of Christ himself. It is another dark tone thrown on to the shadow of Christian ambiguity. But these ambiguities are intrinsic to Christian history, they are a constant part of the burden Christ bears, and it is appropriate that they should be particularly focused on the sacrament that proclaims his death till he comes.

The same ambiguities abound in the sacrament of the pure water which as priests we pour, or into which we gently press our people. We have seen it as the sacrament of new birth, of repentance and the seeking of new life. But we have also seen it abused as a social rite, misunderstood and perverted, yet somehow used by God to prick the longing and the hunger that is there in all of us. And it, too, has been used as an instrument of control, a turnstile to the fount of grace. Christian ministers are frequently driven almost to despair by the dilemmas that face them in the administration of the sacrament of baptism. Some emphasize the solemn nature of the promises and acts of faith and repentance that have always been a part of the ceremony, and feel bound to exclude those whose hold on Christian faith is uncertain or incoherent. Others see the request for baptism as itself a sign of grace and God-hunger and refuse to judge its integrity. If the doctrine of the self-emptying of God in Christ and Christ's surrender of himself to the logic of the divine generosity is at the heart of the Christian mystery, as this book has tried to show, then we must allow God to risk himself in his sacraments, no less than in the crucifixion. We must resist the temptation to act as bodyguards for a God who chooses to express himself in weakness and is found in the fashion of a slave. God, apparently, refuses to take care of himself; he allows himself to be exploited; it is part of the nature of his being that he should do so. The Church's administration of the sacraments should reflect the insane generosity of God, rather than the fear and defensiveness of the Church. God insists on casting his pearls before swine, and we have no right to lock them up in a bank vault.

The sacrament that best captures both the power and elusiveness of God's approach to us is the sacrament of healing. Christ healed and he commanded his Church to follow his example, and it has in a variety of ways. It helped to pioneer and develop scientific medicine and it still prays for and supports the work of hospitals, but it understands something of the mystery of human nature and the interconnectedness of body, mind and spirit. That is why we have a specific sacrament of healing, by prayer, anointing and the laying-on of hands. However, we make an old distinction between curing and healing, between removing the symptoms of disease and bringing peace and wholeness to a person, healing of the spirit. Sometimes they go together, sometimes they don't, but the sacrament of healing always conveys the strength of God in our weakness. We all suffer from the incurable disease of mortality, but we are constantly strengthened in our weakness by the presence of God. And just as the surgeons who minister to us in hospital and mend our ills are themselves human and therefore frail, so also the healers who minister spiritual strength to us are wounded and needy, yet through their weakness the strength of God is mediated.

The Church, its ministers and its sacraments are means of encounter with the divine, though they are themselves far from divine. The holy comes through them, though it is not exclusively contained *within* them. We should come to Church neither with inflated expectations, nor with a dismissive or contemptuous attitude: we should bring to it a reverent scepticism and a sort of sceptical reverence. But we should still come to it expectantly, open to surprise, to the sudden shock of the divine; above all, we should bring this attitude to our worship, to which we so often come unexpectant, without excitement or sense of eager anticipation. God is known here, found here, encountered here; he wrestles with us and we with him; he creeps out upon us, sometimes filling us with loneliness and a longing for him, because all we sense is his absence; sometimes flooding us with the joy of his presence. Powerful places are our churches, powerful with loss and powerful with longing, powerful with prayers poured out in pain and suffering. I am always very moved by Intercession Boards in churches, places to which people bring their longings and heartaches – "for Gwen suffering from cancer; for John in depression; for Mary and Ian whose marriage is in difficulties; for a young woman with anorexia; for a boy who has made three attempts to take his own life; for Jim dying of AIDS; that I might find faith; that God would show me how to serve him, to help me break a bad and destructive relationship; that I might overcome alcoholism; that I might find faith; for the people of Ethiopia, El Salvador, Northern Ireland" – all the need, joy and anguish of humanity, all brought on bits of paper and placed on the altar of God. Who can tell what is wrought by that poignant ritual?

Ambiguities are forever, and they are in *us* as well as in the Church. A bit of us is faithful, a bit of us is untrue; a bit of us is longing, a bit of us is cynical; a bit of us wants to give more, a bit of us want to give up; a bit of us wants to make the effort, a bit of us can't be bothered. Yes, ambiguities are forever. If we come to church humbly, humble in ourselves and humble in our expectations, God will meet us; but only if we learn to look deeply, to penetrate beneath the obvious to the divinity veiled in the sign.

> Faith our outward sense befriending
> makes the inward vision clear.[1]

7

JUDGEMENT

... where their worm does not die,
and the fire is not quenched. (Mark
9:48)

The part of the scripture that presents the gravest difficulty
for modern Christians is the teaching on judgement, hell and
the return of Christ to earth. The problem lies in coming
to terms with the world view that lies behind ancient
documents that are still spiritually relevant. The difficulty
is always how to separate the kernel from the husk. There
is a well-known danger here, often commented upon by
conservative-minded Christians, of throwing away the baby
with the bath water. But we all live with this problem. Even
those who *claim* to take the whole of scripture literally, in
fact never do so. They always operate on some principle
of selection, however ambiguously or unconsciously. But
the problem we are dealing with in this chapter is not about
rival interpretations of scripture, or even about the nature
of its authority. Such disputes are endless. Our task is a more
immediate but more modest one. It is to give some account
of how Christians, who would describe themselves as
modern believers, might handle this kind of material. By
modern believers, I mean those who genuinely believe in and
try to follow the way of Christ, but who are inescapably
contemporary in their outlook and assumptions, even though

they know that many of these assumptions are likely to be flawed and inadequate. We can only believe as we are able, if we are to be honest with ourselves, and for many modern followers of Jesus the part of the scripture that talks about hell presents serious difficulties. The difficulties arise because we want to take Jesus and the New Testament seriously, but we find enormous conflict between our own liberal sentiments on the punishment of sinners and the language of the New Testament.

Before addressing the subject, it is important to remember that most of the elaborations of the image of hell are not from the New Testament, but are medieval developments of the theme, sometimes based on traditions in early Judaism. What is said in the New Testament is sparing. It will be of some help if we look at two specific texts and try to come to some preliminary understanding of them:

If your hand causes you to sin, cut it off; it is better for you to enter life maimed than with two hands to go to hell, to the unquenchable fire. (Mark 9:43–44)

There was a rich man, who was clothed in purple and fine linen and who feasted sumptuously every day. And at his gate lay a poor man named Lazarus, full of sores, who desired to be fed with what fell from the rich man's table: moreover the dogs came and licked his sores. The poor man died and was carried by the angels to Abraham's bosom. The rich man also died and was buried; and in Hades, being in torment, he lifted up his eyes, and saw Abraham far off and Lazarus in his bosom. And he called out, "Father Abraham, have mercy upon me, and send Lazarus to dip the end of his finger in water and cool my tongue; for I am in anguish in this flame." But Abraham said, "Son, remember that you in your lifetime received your good things, and Lazarus in like manner evil things; but now he is comforted here, and you are in anguish. And besides all this, between us and you a great chasm has been fixed, in order that those who would pass from here to you may not be able and none may cross from there to us." And he said, "Then I beg you, father, to send him to my father's house for I have five brothers, so that he may warn them, lest they also come into this place of torment." But Abraham said, "They have Moses and the prophets; let them hear them." And he said, "No, father Abraham; but if some one goes to them from the dead, they will repent." He said to him, "If they do not hear Moses and the prophets, neither will they be convinced if some one should rise from the dead." (Luke 16:19–31)

The Mark passage is a good example of Jesus' method of operation. He was a first-century Jew who accepted and used the world view and culture of his day; and part of the theological furniture of the time was the conviction that the sins of this life were purged or burned away after death. However, it is dangerous to be too precise here, because Jesus is also speaking metaphorically. In this verse he uses the word *gehenna* for hell, a place which we know something about. Gehenna was originally the valley of Hinnom on the south side of Jerusalem, where child sacrifice had once been offered to the god, Moloch.

Ahaz was twenty years old when he began to reign, and he reigned sixteen years in Jerusalem. And he did not do what was right in the eyes of the Lord, like his father

David, but walked in the ways of the kings of Israel. He even made molten images for the Baals; and he burned incense in the valley of the son of Hinnom, and burned his sons as an offering, according to the abominable practises of the nations whom the Lord drove out before the people of Israel. (2 Chronicles 28:1–3)

At a later date the place became the city's refuse dump, where rubbish was burned. It was, indeed, a place where the worm did not die and the fire was never quenched. By the time of Jesus it had become a metaphor for the state of sinners after death. In this verse, therefore, we can be confident that Jesus was not speculating about the exact nature of the afterlife; rather he was taking for granted the world view of his hearers and was using it to point to a spiritual reality. He was getting at the danger of unrepented sin. Jesus always addressed this subject with great urgency; it is an indelible part of his message. But it is important to keep the focus upon the challenge to us to repent, rather than upon the picture of our state after death. The focus is not upon hell, but upon the consequences of unrepented sin.

A similar background is found in the Lukan parable. Some commentators believe that this story had an independent circulation and was not an original creation by Jesus. It is possible that he used it in his own way by giving a particular interpretation to it. Jesus had a vivid method of teaching, which made use of what was to hand, whether it was a recent incident, a well-known architectural folly or a familiar story. Again, we can be confident that the story was not designed to give people a detailed picture of the afterstate of an uncaring man, because we can safely assume that Jesus' hearers would already be familiar with this view of things.

The point of the parable is to remind us of the duties of life, not to satisfy our curiosity about our state after death. In other words, Jesus assumed the reality of hell for teaching purposes, very much in the way a modern preacher might use our knowledge of the dangers to the ozone layer and the overheating of the environment as contemporary examples of human delinquency. Preachers always preach from within a world view; they do not preach the world view, but they use it to bring their listeners to spiritual awareness.

The world view or cosmology of a first-century Jew was what is called the 'wedding-cake' or three-tier universe, with heaven above, earth in the middle and the underworld or place of the dead in the bottom tier. It has often been observed that the New Testament writers, as well as many preachers today, use this language, even though they are well aware that it is essentially metaphorical. To talk of heaven as being *above* is appropriate, because it suggests the transcendent; and talk of the state of those dwelling far from God in unrepented sin, will inescapably lead to the use of words like *under, below, depth, dungeon* or *abyss*. All language about spiritual things is unavoidably metaphorical, but only an obtuse person would fail to realize that a metaphor genuinely *conveys* meaning and truth, though not in a literalistic way. Talk of God as *father* is metaphor, however sacred it is to Christians. It suggests an attitude of care and strength, of protectiveness and authority, rather than the possession of specific masculine characteristics. Similarly, pictures from the Old Testament of the Holy Spirit hovering like a great bird over the waters and breathing life into them are powerfully and evocatively metaphorical; as is the picture of God using his hands to mould the first man from the clay of the earth. We need not fear the knowledge that the language of the spirit is metaphorical and analogical. Jesus was a master of metaphor and simile. He taught through parables, and the word parable is the same word as *parabola*, something thrown over something else, like the rope that a cowboy throws round the neck of a steer. A parable lassoes an external event and pulls it into divine use. In the same way, Jesus took for granted certain conventions, both political and theological, and he delivered his challenge to people within that structure of understanding.

In the Judaism of our Lord's day there had been a heightening and a developing of what we might call a 'compensatory eschatology'. One of the best ways to understand this phenomenon is to look at a more modern version of the same thing, from the history of slavery. The African slaves in the USA, in their pain and bondage, developed a 'compensatory' theology of heaven and hell to console them in their misery and to satisfy their own sense of the justice of God. African-American music from the days of slavery, and from the days of wage-slavery to the plantation boss that followed abolition, is filled with longing for heaven. Something similar happened to Judaism in the period between the writing of the Old and New Testaments. This small but proud and godly nation found itself endlessly crushed between rival empires. Part of the response was the development of what is call 'apocalyptic', an untidy set of fantasies and expectations, in which God vindicated his children by punishing their oppressors. As with common notions of life after death, this was no systematic theory but a series of visions, some of which related to the punishment of oppressors, and some of which related to a historical vindication of the Jewish people by the coming of a great leader, the Son of Man, who would judge the nations and reign for a thousand years, before the great battles that would finally vindicate the righteousness of God.

Traces of these apocalyptic yearnings are found in the New Testament, most noticeably in the book of Revelation; but they are also found in the utterances of Jesus and are part of the mental furniture that he used. It has always been difficult for interpreters of Jesus to separate the essentials elements of his message and purpose from their incidental additions. If we accept the premise of a specific incarnation of God in a historical event or through a historical personage, it will be obvious that the vehicle of the revelation will itself assume a certain significance, by association with the divine visitation. This is the same dynamic that evolves from reverence for objects associated with worship and sacrament into an almost magical superstition, whereby the vessels and garments associated with the sanctuary become themselves identified as holy. It is an inevitable but misleading process, and it should be subjected to rigorous criticism. God may come through an event or a person, but it is spiritually deadening, however humanly understandable, to allow our weakness for magic to cast a spell over every detail in the revelatory event. If God was in Jesus of Nazareth, a first-century man, and if he was truly human, as well as a means of divine revelation, then he must have operated within the given circumstances of his time. We know that he was a Jew, circumcised on the eighth day; that he lived a circumscribed life in an area never more than a hundred miles from Jerusalem. Spiritual genius though he was, he was of necessity a creature of his time, and he used the language and culture of his day in teaching a new understanding of the nature of God.

The most conspicuous example of the way in which an uncritical acceptance of first-century norms has bedevilled theological development is the ordination of women. It is not our purpose to debate the issue here, but it is worth noting that the core of the argument against the ordination of women is that Jesus did not choose women to be apostles or leaders in his community. It is also recognized, of course, that to have done so would have been an extraordinary departure from the norms of his society, so extraordinary as to be counter-productive. Nevertheless, are we, living in a very different type of society, still to be conformed to the social norms of Jerusalem in the first century? To say that we must is to give the culture of the society into which Christ came as much authority as the core of the revealed truth itself. If we take this approach, then we replace the God of history, the God known in time and its successiveness, with the God of the time-warp, the God who arbitrarily sacralizes a single era in cultural history, with all its accidents and confusions, and bestows upon it some kind of final significance.

If, on the other hand, we recognize that the God who is known to us in history and who continues to lead us through it, has expressed himself uniquely in a single life, whose significance we must continue to interpret for our own time, then we are committed to a dangerous business, because there is an element of judgement and finality in the message and person of Christ that brings all cultures and traditions under its authority. Nevertheless, we are faced with the inescapable duty of discerning the essential from the incidental, the eternal message from its temporal trappings.

This business of interpretation is not an exact science, but most men and women of sound judgement and common sense will understand the broad distinction and have little difficulty in separating the heart of the message from its first-century context. We must see the message of Jesus as a whole; we must not flinch from the severe side of his words and his deeds. Holiness is costly, and God calls us to holiness for the sake of our own happiness. But the fundamental nature of the message is a call to life, to joy and to fulfilment. God has not booby-trapped the universe in order to tease his confused creatures. He calls us through time to eternity, because he longs for our fulfilment.

Perhaps the most vivid example of this overwhelming tenderness and mercy is found in the story of the penitent thief:

One of the criminals who were hanged railed at him, saying, "Are you not the Christ? Save yourself and us!" But the other rebuked him, saying, "Do you not fear God, since you are under the same sentence of condemnation? And we indeed justly; for we are receiving the due reward of our deeds; but this man has done nothing wrong." And he said, "Jesus remember me when you come into your kingdom." And he said to him, "Truly, I say to you, today you will be with me in Paradise." (Luke 23:39–43)

That brief access of pity by the thief, who probably thought he was consoling a deluded maniac who imagined himself to be king, was instantly met by the grace of the God who wants to affirm what is best in us and rescue us from our own ignorant destructiveness.

The use of the idea of hell in later theological and social

history parallels much else that we have noticed about the way the followers of Christ have twisted his radical doctrine of the way of unpower and unforce into the way of domination. Hell has been instrumentalized and made into a means of control over individuals and societies. A metaphor used by our Lord as a direct challenge to the individual to mind the lateness of the hour, is turned into an instrument of terror, for the *scaring* of people into a kingdom that Christ died to give them. One of the most famous examples of this abuse of the concept of hell comes in James Joyce's *Portrait of the Artist as a Young Man*, where he recalls a sermon in which the torments of hell were described with an ugly relish:

> The torment of fire is the greatest torment to which the tyrant has ever subjected his fellow creatures. Place your finger for a moment in the flame of a candle and you will feel the pain of fire. But our earthly fire was created by God for the benefit of man, to maintain in him the spark of life and to help him in the useful arts, whereas the fire of hell is of another quality and was created by God to torture and punish the unrepentant sinner. Our earthly fire also consumes more or less rapidly according as the object which it attacks is more or less combustible, so that human ingenuity has even succeeded in inventing chemical preparations to check or frustrate its action. But the sulphurous brimstone which burns in hell is a substance which is specially designed to burn for ever and for ever with unspeakable fury. Moreover, our earthly fire destroys at the same time as it burns, so that the more intense it is the shorter is its duration; but the fire of hell has this property, that it preserves that which

it burns, and, though it rages with incredible intensity, it rages for ever.

Our earthly fire again, no matter how fierce or widespread it may be, is always of a limited extent; but the lake of fire in hell is boundless, shoreless and bottomless. And this terrible fire will not afflict the bodies of the damned only from without but each lost soul will be a hell unto itself, the boundless fire raging in its very vitals. O, how terrible is the lot of those wretched beings! The blood seethes and boils in the veins, the brains are boiling in the skull, the heart in the breast glowing and bursting, the bowels a red-hot mass of burning pulp, the tender eyes flaming like molten balls.[1]

In addition to the use of hell as an instrument of social control has gone something more subtle, which seems to reflect forces in our own unconscious. All our searching for God is, to a great extent, done in our own minds and souls, so it is inevitably a potent mixture of divine longing and human neurosis. We know that there is a high level of unavoidable projection going on in the spiritual process. Indeed, some thinkers dismiss *all* religion as having no reality beyond its origins in the human struggle to understand life and find something to live for. There can be little doubt that human beings have projected much of their own self-hatred and anger on to God, as well as whole ranges of unconscious fears, mysteriously built into us by our share in the memory of peoples and races. Our minds are filled with ugly mysteries as well as good desires and longings. The sexual instinct itself often seems to become a focus for this tendency to distort and disfigure our own goodness. One of the elements in our own society that we are feeling increasingly shocked and puzzled by is the sexual abuse of young children, sometimes ritualistically. It is difficult to account for such brooding evils, except on the hypothesis that there are forces in reality that seem to plug into our unconscious and, if the conditions are ripe, flood us with cruelty and ugliness.

In addition to the sexual manifestation of these terrible forces, we must recognize the racial examples; and if we roll the film in our mind it can quickly fill with horrifying images of persecution and racialist fury. We find examples of this in scripture, which never shirks from showing us unacceptable reflections of ourselves and our doctrines of God. It is not surprising, therefore, that creatures like us produce ideas like hell and use them as instruments of terror. Nevertheless, it is unwise to take a first-century myth, used by our Lord because it was part of the mind-set of the era, though never finally or fully articulated, and turn it into an article of faith, complete with a detailed, Dantean map of its horrors.

But how are we to use this material? The obvious answer is to point to the use our Lord made of it as a reminder of the inevitability of judgement. If the universe has a moral structure and a divine author, then his purposes must be vindicated and righteousness must be shown to be right. This was the burden of Jesus' call to us to repent. The word 'repent' has many resonances, but its broadest meaning is a call to men and women to change their minds around, to see things straight. We cannot live our lives dishonestly and face the God of truth without pain. We can only enter eternal life, the life that is life indeed, on the basis of an honest acceptance of what we have made of ourselves. The problem here is nothing to do with moral outrage on the part of God, or any desire in God to punish us; but it has everything to do with reality, including our own personal reality. This is a truth that many modern psychological therapies recognize. Just as modern management techniques are turning to the collaborative and associational model of human relationships commended by our Lord, so modern techniques for dealing with the various types of self-destructive behaviour use methods of radical confrontation, because they know there can be no true healing except on the basis of honest acknowledgement of our estate. They issue a call to repentance: "Unless you, John Doe, admit to this kind of behaviour and agree that you no longer have control over it, but that it controls you, you will inhabit a hell of increasing and unceasing misery." This is extreme rhetoric, but it is a realistic challenge to the human situation. Groups like Alcoholics Anonymous know the therapeutic power of such radical honesty: "My name is John and I am an alcoholic" is a healing act of repentance, of *metanoia;* and all of us have to make these acts of self-owning. We must face the truth about ourselves; judgement is reality.

Questions about the state after death of unrepentant sinners are interesting but unanswerable. It is inconceivable that the God of mercy should create a realm of eternal punishment, but it is conceivable that sin eternally unrepented could keep us from God. But we must not fall into the trap of developing this idea in a falsely elaborate way. Hell is not a space but a state of mind. The vast literature on adultery, for instance, shows that a man who is secretly unfaithful to his wife is unable to enjoy an honest relationship with her and may be said to be in a hell of guilt and discomfort, as long as he maintains the deception. There is powerful metaphorical truth in the idea of hell and eternal burning, because shame and guilt can burn into our very souls and destroy our peace of mind: but it is this very burning that Jesus wishes to rescue us from, not plunge us into. Jesus came to *rescue* us from hell; and it is the most scandalous of all the paradoxes of Christian history that the Christ who wanted to rescue us from the pain of our own dishonesty and self-hatred has been used by Christian leaders and teachers as a bogeyman and figure of terror. All he ever wanted to say to us was, "Today you will be with me in paradise."

The other major element in the New Testament, already touched on, that is likely to be baffling to the modern believer, is 'apocalyptic', from the Greek word to uncover or reveal. Common to all apocalyptic thought is a vision of the end time, usually preceded by a time of great turmoil and tribulation, after which there will be a great coming in glory of a heavenly figure who will bring the nations to judgement and establish his followers in positions of authority. The most concentrated example of this strand in the New Testament is probably found in Mark's Gospel, in chapter 13:

> But when you see the desolating sacrilege set up where it ought not to be (let the reader understand), then let those who are in Judea flee to the mountains; let him who is on the housetop not go down, nor enter his house, to take anything away; and let him who is in the field not turn back to take his mantle. And alas for those who are with child and for those who give suck in those days! Pray that it may not happen in winter. For in those days there will be such tribulation as has not been from the beginning of the creation which God created until now, and never will be. And if the Lord had not shortened the days, no

141

human being would be saved; but for the sake of the elect, whom he chose, he shortened the days. And then if any one says to you, "Look, here is the Christ!" or "Look, there he is!" do not believe it. False Christs and false prophets will arise and show signs and wonders, to lead astray, if possible, the elect. But take heed; I have told you all things beforehand.

But in those days, after that tribulation, the sun will be darkened, and the moon will not give its light, and the stars will be falling from heaven, and the powers in the heavens will be shaken. And then they will see the Son of man coming in clouds with great power and glory. And then he will send out the angels, and gather his elect from the four winds, from the ends of the earth to the ends of heaven. (Mark 13:14–27)

We have already noticed in our discussion of the concept of hell that Jesus of Nazareth was a man of his time, who had unavoidably absorbed the world view of his contemporaries. In many ways it is easier to come to terms with the overall outline of the first-century pre-scientific view of creation, than with its more esoteric longings for the future that we find in apocalyptic literature. There are strong traces of apocalyptic expectation in scripture and they conditioned the early Church into expecting the imminent return of Jesus. It is difficult to rate the value of these passages in our contemporary task of interpreting the New Testament, but they do raise a fundamental issue that is troublesome for Christians who have a too static view of the perfection of Christ. If we take these predictions as coming literally from the mouth of Jesus, and as having a clear meaning, then we have to admit that he was mistaken. Two thousand years after his crucifixion he has still not returned in glory, in the manner outlined in the predictions, and the Church has largely come to terms with the fact. For a person with a robust and intelligent faith, the fact that Jesus was mistaken about this will not be a major problem, especially if we accept the argument of the previous pages.

We shall probably also have to admit to a great deal of bafflement in dealing with this material, or in finding contemporary uses for its. It is firmly set in a particular and highly complex tradition, into whose mentality it is difficult for most of us to enter. One honest way to deal with the material, therefore, is simply to be baffled by it, though we can all respond to the poetic anguish that it reveals and can identify ways in which it is an uncannily accurate description of many episodes in history, including some in the recent past. There have been some thinkers who have seen apocalyptic as the main clue to interpreting Jesus and they have been forced thereby to see him as an ultimately despairing figure. Convinced that the New Age was about to be born, and convinced also of his own crucial role in bringing it to pass, he plays his hand; but God does not respond and he dies in despair. The most eloquent statement of this position is found in Albert Schweitzer's classic work, *The Quest of the Historical Jesus* where he writes:

> There is silence all around. The Baptist appears, and cries: "Repent for the Kingdom of Heaven is at hand." Soon after that comes Jesus, and in the knowledge that He is the coming Son of Man lays hold of the wheel of the world to set it moving on that last revolution which is to bring all ordinary history to a close. It refuses to turn, and He throws Himself upon it. Then it does turn; and crushes

Him. Instead of bringing in the eschatological conditions, He has destroyed them. The wheel rolls onward, and the mangled body of the one immeasurably great Man, who was strong enough to think of Himself as the spiritual ruler of mankind and to bend history to His purpose, is hanging upon it still. That is His victory and His reign.[2]

That is one way of resolving the issue and it has enormous emotional power, but it has not commended itself to all interpreters and it seems to be contradicted by the fact of the Resurrection, which is the basis of all subsequent Christian experience. Looking back at this material from our side of the Resurrection, how are we to use it? How are we to interpret it? We must begin by acknowledging that men and women have always been fascinated by the future. This accounts for the continued interest in the occult and in various types of future-gazing or prediction, such as astrology and Tarot. There have been many ways of future-gazing, such as palmistry or the crystal ball. The ancient art of haruspication sought knowledge of the future by the discovery of signs in the entrails of slaughtered chickens. In the street I grew up in there were one or two old ladies who practised the ancient art of reading tea leaves. The Church has always looked disapprovingly on this phenomenon and has sometimes tried to have it banned by society; but there is little doubt that human beings will continue to have an intense curiosity about their future, for two main reasons.

First, we all experience a fundamental uncertainty as we face the future. Who knows what might befall us? Our present happiness is a very slender thread that can be broken in an instant. A blood vessel bursts in the brain of someone we dearly love, and the thread is broken. A driver has one whisky too many and a young life we adore is destroyed on some grim roadway, and the thread is broken. Someone we thought to be true and steadfast turns from us and changes joy into misery, and the thread is broken. These things happen daily to people we know. They could happen to us. So we are all, in one way or another, faced with a fundamental uncertainty as we gaze towards the future. If we are not careful the uncertainty can lead to a morbid anxiety that can destroy our ability to enjoy the present. We are interested in the future, therefore, because it threatens us.

But along with this uncertainty about the future goes something else. There is in all of us a need to look forward. We all seem to need something to live for, some hope that lies ahead, some promised fulfilment, some event, however trivial. This need to look forward can take many forms. Most of us spend a lot of time looking to and planning for the future. This is especially true of children, who are always looking forward: to Christmas, to the holidays, to birthdays, to growing up. But none of us ever loses this characteristic. In a most extraordinary way we live towards the future, constantly looking ahead, if only to our next day off or visit to the theatre. We all need something out there, ahead of us, a special attraction, "a future presentation", as they say at the cinema, "coming next week in glorious technicolour", something to look forward to. We are interested in the future because it can be full of promise.

All of this adds up to two very simple needs: we want to be secure, free from threat; and we want to be happy. That is why the future tantalizes us: it is both threat and promise. Who knows what it will bring? Will it be the oil of gladness or the ashes of mourning, the garland of praise or the spirit of heaviness? What will it be? Is life simply a gamble, a game of chance in which some win and some lose; some find happiness and some find misery, with no rhyme or reason to it? Is there no certainty to which we can hold, no ground on which we can stand?

On one level the answer to that question must be "No", however quietly and fearfully we whisper it to ourselves. There is no certainty in this life; there is nothing we can lay hold of and say, "This, at least, will never be taken from me", for all things pass away. There is no life, no joy that is not subject to the terrible law of change and decay. Every summer fades into winter and all the leaves fall. There is nothing in this life that can bear forever the weight of our hope; if we lean upon it too heavily, then sooner or later it will snap like a dry stick. Even the happiest and most fulfilled marriage ends in death, as an old poem testifies:

> A little way to walk with you, my own,
>   Only a little way;
> Then one of us must weep and walk alone
>   Until God's day.

The combination of uncertainty and eagerness – uncertainty about what lies in store for us, and eagerness to have something to look forward to – is a potent combination in the human imagination. We spend a lot of time both in anxious imaginings and in pleasant imaginings. We can be anxious about our health or the safety and welfare of those we love; and we often day-dream, especially but not exclusively when we are young, about love or fame or happy-ever-afterness. We are born gazing into the future. We seem

146

to find it necessary to live ahead of ourselves, looking into the distance for something or someone to come into our lives. When I tell my in-laws in the USA that I shall be able to visit them on one of my working trips, my ninety-year-old father-in-law always expresses great eagerness: "It'll give me something to look forward to," he says.

This business of looking forward, gazing ahead into the mists of the future, is an important element in human nature and it is a profound element in religion and politics, as well as in our private lives. We are constituted to look ahead to some great thing. There's a song in *West Side Story* that sums it up, and it captures something of the bitter-sweet nature of human longings:

I've got a feeling there's a miracle due, gonna come true,
    Comin' to me.
    Can it be? Yes it will
    Maybe just by holdin' still
    It'll be there . . .
Come on something, Come on in,
    Don't be shy
    Meet a guy
    Draw up a chair
The air is hummin'
And something great is comin' . . .[3]

As we have seen, looking forward to some great visitation by God or the return of Christ is a potent element in Christian history. We can expect a heightening of this as we move towards the close of the millennium, but fascination with the future will always be there. History is filled with examples of men and women who confidently claimed to know the precise pattern of the uncertain future; they knew when the end would be, when the mighty thing would come to pass.

I grew up in a small place in the west of Scotland and I remember one week a stranger came to town. He started walking the streets wearing sandwich-boards on which were written: "The end is nigh". He had come to announce the end of the world and the day of the Lord, and he was quite specific about his message: all would end at 2 p.m. on Friday afternoon. It so happened that I had a particularly grim piece of maths homework to prepare for that very hour. I decided that there was little point in doing it, since we'd all be preoccupied by other matters at that very time. I didn't do my homework, but nor did the day of the Lord arrive. The maths teacher was not prepared to accept preparation for the end of the world as a valid excuse for cutting homework, and I was severely belted at the very moment when the end was supposed to occur. Maybe the prophet was closer to the mark than we all thought.

Predictions about the end of the world and the return of Christ are so specific in the New Testament that, as we have seen, the first Christians were in daily expectation of his return. A lot of them seem to have spent their time lying around waiting, seeing little point in starting anything that would end so soon. Paul had to get firm with some of them in Thessalonica, warning them that if they were going to give up working in order to wait for the return of the Lord, then they ought to give up eating too: "If a man will not work, let him not eat," he said. As the end did not come, the Christians became adjusted to their situation and settled down to the long haul of history, living between the first coming of Christ and his promised return, but seeking to live so that they would be ready whenever he did return. Throughout Christian history there have been groups who have predicted the Second Coming on the basis either of private revelations or because they claim to have discovered a mysterious message in scripture which they have decoded. Several best-selling books in fundamentalist circles confidently predict the end of all things in the very near future. Predictions of this sort are common in a turbulent time, because they seem to conform to the biblical predictions of the distress and tribulations of the last days.

What spiritual use can we make of this mysterious element in the holy scriptures that locks on to our human need to look forward? We must note, first of all, that even in the New Testament we find a development of ideas on the subject. John, for instance, seems to teach that the Day of the Lord has already come:

Now is the judgement of this world, now shall the ruler of this world be cast out. (John 12:31)

And this is eternal life, that they know thee the only true God, and Jesus Christ whom thou hast sent. (17:3)

This is what some theologians call 'realized eschatology': the final act of God has already occurred. We are now living through the last times. *These* are the last days. The Resurrection of Jesus was the Second Coming, and we are living in the final scene of the last act of history. Even now we can have an eternal and saving relationship with Jesus Christ. "*Now* is the day of judgement", whether we acknowledge it or not.

A second approach has been to apply the doctrine of the

Second Coming or the Day of the Lord to the certainty of our own death. We are always old enough to die, and death is the one certain fact of our existence: "Remember, man, that dust thou art, and unto dust shalt thou return." We must live, therefore, so that we can face our Maker at a moment's notice. The Day of the Lord is nearer than we think. We must live so that we will not be ashamed in that day. We must redeem the time, buy back the time we have wasted, with deeper seriousness and care.

This was the biblical note that converted the dissolute Augustine of Hippo. He was sitting moodily in a garden one afternoon, filled with self-loathing and confusion at the state of his life, watching it trickle away in insignificance, when he heard a child's voice crying, *"Tolle, lege, tolle, lege"* – "Take and read, take and read." He picked up the Christian scriptures, which he had been desultorily reading, and opened them at random and came immediately upon the great passage in Romans:

> Let us conduct ourselves becomingly as in the day, not in revelling and drunkenness, not in debauchery and licentiousness, not in quarrelling and jealousy. But put on the Lord Jesus Christ, and make no provision for the flesh, to gratify its desires. (Romans 13:13–14)

And he stood up and walked into history as one of the greatest Christians of all time. Meditation upon the shortness of life and the certainty of death can marvellously concentrate our minds, so that we turn away from the trivial and wasteful, the sordid and selfish, and place the whole energy of our life into the control and direction of Christ.

And there is a third approach. We find it in the parable

of the talents, where our Lord implies that there is a deliberately planned delay in his return:

> For it will be as a man going on a journey called his servants and entrusted to them his property; to one he gave five talents, to another two, to another one, to each according to his ability. Then he went away. (Matthew 25:14–15)

This is the beginning of the famous parable of the talents. A talent was worth a significant sum of money, so the king left a small fortune with each of his servants, and went on a journey in order to test their certainty of purpose and energy of soul. "Use those talents", he told them, "make them grow." This suggest that the time between our Lord's first coming and his second is for our sake. He delivers his cause into our hands. He leaves with us the enormous treasure of the Christian faith and the Universal Church and asks us to make them grow, to spread them, to increase his investment. His anger was reserved for the man who simply kept the faith to himself, who hid it in the ground and did nothing with it. The implication is obvious: according to the measure of our gifts and ability, we are to labour for the spreading of God's kingdom on earth, while we wait for his second coming in majesty. At that coming, we will be examined not only on the moral and spiritual consequences of the way we have lived, but on our record as evangelists, as investors of the Lord's treasure. Most of us are too shy and fastidious to be effective evangelists. But we don't have to be bores, or spiritual vulgarians to be evangelists, spreaders of the good news. If each Christian made a point of introducing one friend a year to the Church, there would be an amazing increase in the influence of Jesus Christ in the world, not to mention the joy and spiritual strength that would develop in the persons brought there. There are many ways in which to make these gentle introductions. There are many people in our society who want to meet Jesus, who long for new purpose in their lives, who are spiritually hungry. All we are called upon to do is make the introduction and let the friendship happen, but we are called upon to do at least that.

So the theme of Christ's return gives us much to think about. It is a reality we face now: we are standing before Christ all the day long; he calls us now – what is our response? It is a reality we shall clearly face at death, when the secrets of all hearts will be revealed – live, then, so as not to be ashamed in that day.

Meanwhile, we are to live with confidence and purpose. We are to fulfil our time, make use of it to enlarge the meaning of our own life and the mission of the Church. The message is, "Keep calm and keep the faith", put excellently in a memory from the American Revolution recounted by Alistair Cooke in a recent lecture:

The time was the 19 May 1780. The place was Hartford, Connecticut. The day has gone down in New England history as a terrible foretaste of Judgement Day. For at noon the skies turned from blue to grey and by midafternoon had blackened over so densely that, in that religious age, men fell on their knees and begged a final blessing before the end came. The Connecticut House of Representatives was in session. And as some men fell down and others clamoured for an immediate adjournment, the Speaker of the House, one Colonel

Davenport, came to his feet. He silenced them and said these words:

"The Day of Judgement is either approaching or it is not. If it is not, there is no cause for adjournment. If it is, I choose to be found doing my duty. I wish, therefore, that candles may be brought."[4]

8

MEANWHILE

... you have sorrow now, but I will see you again. (John 16:22)

E.M. Forster talked about "poor little talkative Christianity", and one knows exactly what he meant. Christianity often seems to be drowning in words. Years ago a pen-and-ink drawing was on display in one of the rooms at Iona Abbey, showing a large thick-set man in a pulpit, and falling out of his mouth and piling up on the pulpit and on the floor beside it was a flow of words, words, words, words. Christianity is a very 'wordy' religion and its history is filled with the clash of debate, as we have argued about our interpretation of the central event that dominates our history. Unfortunately, it is very easy to keep Christianity in the head and treat it as a matter of theories and propositions. It can be thought of as a body of knowledge that, to some extent, can be mastered from books and from those who teach theology. All of this is fair enough, because in one sense the study of Christian history is a science, a body of knowledge that can be learned; and it can be learned by an atheist quite as skilfully as by a believer. Cardinal Newman pointed out that the unbelieving Gibbon was the best Church historian England has ever produced.

Nevertheless, all of this adds up to a reversal of scripture. According to John, in Christ 'the Word became flesh', idea became personal reality. But in so much Christian experience the flesh becomes *word*, and the personal reality becomes abstract theory. It is important to remember, therefore, that Christianity is not a perfectly rounded theory in which everything finds a place, as in, for example, Marxism or Freudian analysis, where an over-arching theory answers every problem. Christian teaching is very different. It is fundamentally a reflection on experience. The Christian life is a life lived in experience, a relationship, and as in any relationship there is much muddle, mystery and confusion. This means that Christians learn to live by faith, with many unanswered questions. Nevertheless, though they may not be able to offer rounded explanations for the difficulties that confront them, they do have a duty to wrestle, as well as they are able, with the theoretical consequences of their own belief. And the greatest problem that faces any Christian believer is the problem of suffering, the problem of "the world's ancient sorrow". Let us, in this final chapter, therefore, spill more words on this intractable subject and hope that they won't be too abstract and theoretical.

One day in the early 1970s, when I was a parish priest in Edinburgh, the chaplain of the prison on the Isle of Wight phoned me. He said they had a prisoner due to be released whom he wanted to send as far away from the south of England as possible, and would I help. I said yes, and the ex-prisoner, whom we'll call George, duly arrived on my doorstep in Edinburgh. I had already been given something of his background from the chaplain. I knew that he had been a brilliant accountant, with an established place in society, a wife and family, but that he had lost it all because of a spectacular drinking problem that led him to frequent binges, characterized by a manic grandiosity of behaviour, leading him into debt and crime. He had been imprisoned for rifling telephone boxes and other acts of larceny in London, while sleeping rough on the Embankment. He walked into my life with a broad smile and a firm handshake. He was tall, elegant, well-dressed, with a bowler hat and a prison haircut. He soon settled down in Edinburgh and found himself a job as an accountant in a well-established Edinburgh firm. With one of those comic ironies that littered his life, he was sent to the Highlands to do his first audit at a whisky distillery. The inevitable happened and one of the partners had to drive up to the hotel where he was staying and bring him back to Edinburgh to dry out. That was the beginning of a roller-coaster that ran for several years. The pattern was always the same: George would get a good job, because he was a brilliant man with impeccable qualifications; he would work well for a month or two and then go on a spectacular bender; he would come to my home to dry out; our parishioners would pray hard for him and he would receive the laying-on of hands; and soon he bounced back to temporary sobriety. Then the pattern speeded up and he started breaking the law seriously. One Easter, three years after his first appearance in our midst, he left Edinburgh for the south. A few weeks later I was informed that he had been found dead on Brighton beach, though it took some time for his body to be identified. When I heard the news I was filled with a combination of anger and relief.

George's story seemed to me to be a caricature or cartoon of the human condition. There are two elements that contribute to human frailty. There is an objective or external dimension. In George's case, this must include all the circumstances of his life that led him to his apocalyptic style of alcohol abuse. Presumably, some of these forces had to do with early nurture and its failures; possibly his own genetic inheritance, and certainly the reality of a universe that included addictive substances and dangerous companions. In addition to these forces outside the self, there are all the subjective or internal realities that move us. Jesus said that it is not what comes into a man from outside that makes him unclean, but what comes from within the man's own heart. Without offering any explanation, we have to acknowledge some responsibility for our own weaknesses, and for colluding with our own failures and fantasies. But even here there is a certain objectivity, a certain sense in which our hand is dealt to us and we play it out. Human beings seem to inherit a tendency to egocentric irrationality and a bias towards evil, as well as towards good. Our hearts are filled with good desires, as well as selfish longings and a mysterious loneliness that can lead us terribly astray.

These two aspects of the personal environment, internal and external, seem to correspond to the nature of evil itself. Evil is an obvious and unpleasant fact in human history, but accounting for the fact is less straightforward. There are several rival theories, which are partly descriptive and partly philosophical or explanatory. We have already hinted in Chapter One at one way of handling or accounting for the sorrows of history and the evils of creation. If the universe is simply a massive natural fact, with no meaning or purpose, then the existence of pain and sorrow are parts of the fact, aspects of the phenomenon. In this theory there is no attempt to offer a reason for the universe: It just *is*, and we have to accept it. If we wanted to describe it, we might see it, certainly in our part of the universe, as a great and ultimately meaningless food chain, with one species preying upon another and clambering upwards, one upon another. Seen from afar, there is even a kind of symmetry and elegance to the thing, though it may repel us when we see it through the magnifying glass of our own human consciousness.

Another naturalistic theory accounts for evil in history in a more spiritual way, by seeing it as a psychic accumulation of wrong choices and mis-opportunities. This is the psychic or spiritual equivalent of a dense chemical fog emitted by an uncaring factory, polluting the atmosphere for miles around. The theory of psychic pollution would see the accumulation of evil deeds as generating an atmosphere of evil, which infects us and disposes us towards wrong deeds, almost without our consent. And we do know that there is a strong element of conditioning in all behaviour, whether good or bad.

The third theory, which again is partly descriptive and partly a philosophical interpretation, is that there is some sort of supernatural reality in evil, giving it an independent identity and objectivity. We quickly have to move into the realm of myth here, but there has been a conviction among human beings for many centuries that the existence of evil is due to some great act of disobedience, some supernatural calamity, some pre-cosmic conspiracy against good. The consequence is that our world is flawed or bent.

However we account for it, evil is experienced as something that exists, in some sense, *apart* from the purely human enterprise. However we explain it, it enlists and influences some part of us that conspires to destroy our own peace; an external force meets an internal force and creates explosions of evil and misery. The roll-call of misery is endless – addiction, disease, violence, depression, nightmarish dreams that breed monstrous realities – real evil.

> And what rough beast, its hour come round at last,
> Slouches towards Bethlehem to be born?[1]

An American psychiatrist, W.Scott Peck, has become persuaded of the existence of objective or supernatural evil, after years of dealing with the tragedies that have come to him. In his book *The People of the Lie*, he catalogues a number of weird examples of evil. One of the most bizarre stories in his catalogue is about a boy who was brought to him by his parents, because he was depressed about his brother's suicide. Dr Peck realized that something hideous was going on, when he discovered that, for his Christmas present that year, the young man had been given by his parents the very rifle with which his brother had blown his brains out.

Subjective evil is easier to analyze but no easier to deal with. On the primary level it seems to be a matter of brutally unavoidable self-centredness. William Temple used to talk about the parable of perspective, by which he meant that each of us sees the world physically from our own centre, quite unavoidably. The universe revolves round me, from where I am within myself. But, of course, it revolves round you in exactly the same way. So the world is filled with colliding egos, all convinced of their own centrality. The purely physical perspective becomes a parable of a more profound psychic and spiritual perspective.

Another side of this is that we can see others clearly, though very imperfectly, but we do not see ourself in the same way, because we would have to unself the self to do that.

159

Really seeing ourselves as others see us requires discipline and honesty, and few of us manage this consistently, so there is inevitably a double standard in operation. We excuse in ourselves behaviour that we can see is clearly unacceptable in others. This accounts for the schizoid nature of evil. It explains all those blatant hypocrisies that characterize us, including the religious among us; the slave traders who were devout Christians; the Nazis who herded the Jews into gas chambers and firing ditches, who were good Catholics or proud Lutherans. If this deception is possible with great and blatant evil, it must obviously be present in subtler, less dramatic evils. And it all results in a profound lack of self-perception. There is in us all a tendency to condemn in others what we excuse in ourselves; we fail to recognize our own state, we live in profound ignorance of our own nature. This is why philosophers tell us that the good life is the examined life. We must grow in self-knowledge, learn to know ourselves and how we operate, before we can be capable of moral progress.

Another element in this formidable complex is the fact of moral impotence. On one level, our difficulty is not one of knowledge. It is not always ignorance of the right thing to do that bothers us. On the whole, in history, something of a general moral consensus has emerged, sometimes formulated in the golden rule, either positively, "Do unto others as you would have them do unto you"; or negatively, "Do not do to others what you would not have them do to you". But one of the real difficulties of the moral life is not in knowing the good but in doing the good, not in identifying the evil, but in avoiding the evil. Paul was the great psychological interpreter of this experience and he has described it in language that all of us can make our own:

I do not understand my own actions. For I do not do what I want, but I do the very thing I hate. Now if I do what I do not want, I agree that the law is good. So then it is no longer I that do it, but sin that dwells within me. For I know that nothing good dwells within me, that is, in my flesh. I can will what is right, but I cannot do it. For I do not do the good I want, but the evil I do not want is what I do. Now if I do what I do not want, it is no longer I that do it, but sin which dwells within me. (Romans 7:15–20)

Human evil in its complex subjective form accumulates into a great force. This clearly has something to do with what psychologists call the 'herd' instinct, which is simply a way of describing the fact that human individuals are often capable of doing evil things in groups that they would avoid, or be in less danger of committing, as private individuals. The collective dimensions seems to remove some element of responsibility and add a powerfully suggestive force, which can remove the individual's own will.

However we account for the fact, either of objective external evil or subjective internal evil, the result is a great power in human history that is ungood and against life. And it seems to have several basic ways of operating. Its single tactical stroke of genius lies in persuading us that instant goods are more desirable than longer lasting goods whose satisfactions are not immediately available. Many of the moral and spiritual dilemmas we get into concentrate round this mysterious competition within our own souls. We know that to fall for the temptation that has presented itself will give us immediate gratification at the expense of long-term peace of mind: this single cigarette will almost certainly trigger off the habit we have spent months programming ourselves against, and bring us back to the old dangers of compulsive smoking; this single drink, after two years on the wagon, may precipitate the final descent into irresponsibility and disease; this sexual act that so tantalizes us may wreck our marriage or destroy our career. We say all these things to ourselves, and we know them to be true. We know that the goods that require the postponement of gratification are longer lasting and more intrinsically satisfying than the quick fixes that lead us to slow misery. But there is something in us that wants to be instantly gratified, no matter the cost, some permanently immature element in our nature, like the baby that calls out in the night for instant solace.

History is filled with examples of these damaging fixes, these fateful one-night stands. One of the most dramatic instances recounted in the Old Testament is the story of David's adultery with Bathsheba. He sees her bathing on the flat rooftop opposite on a sultry evening and is immediately filled with lust for her. He sends for her and exercises his personal charisma and kingly power by seducing her. And the consequences of that night of passion are long-lasting, leading not only to the death of Bathsheba's husband, Uriah the Hittite, but to the very division of the kingdom of Israel. Our newspapers tell frequent stories of shady business practices, short cuts taken in the building of bridges or hotels, that lead to loss of life and the prosecution and imprisonment of the perpetrators. At the base of many of the wrong choices that we make in our lives, and that some of the great and greatly flawed characters in history have made before us, is the urge of instant gratification at the expense of lasting peace.

Meanwhile

The' expense of spirit in a waste of shame
Is lust in action; and, till action, lust
Is perjured, murd'rous, bloody, full of blame,
Savage, extreme, rude, cruel, not to trust;
Enjoyed no sooner but despised straight;
Past reason hunted; and no sooner had,
Past reason hated as a swallowed bait
On purpose laid to make the taker mad;
Mad in pursuit, and in possession so;
Had, having, and in quest to have, extreme;
A bliss in proof, and proved, a very woe.
Before, a joy proposed; behind a dream.
    All this the world well knows; yet none knows well
    To shun the heaven that leads men to this hell.[2]

The power of instant gratification, this desire for immediate pleasure, conspires with a strange inertia or natural sloth in us to militate against moral effort. This conspiracy of sloth and the pleasure principle persuades us over and over again that little or nothing can be done to change the way we are, or the way the universe is. Yeats observed that

> The best lack all conviction, while the worst
> are full of passionate intensity.[3]

We are often stunned into inactivity. We collude with our own feebleness and become morally impotent. We lack the spiritual energy that seeks to grow into maturity, and seeks to change the face of the earth by battling against the great evils that afflict us.

    Yet history shows us again and again that a few energetic souls can do a great deal. We have already noticed that there is an energy of goodness in creation, whether we call it grace, Holy Spirit, or ordinary human kindness, and it can energize us to effect great things and to overturn great evils. This is one of the great themes in scripture, and it assumes many metaphors. There is the famous metaphor of the remnant in Isaiah 10:21: "A remnant will return, the remnant of Jacob, to the mighty God." There are the New Testament metaphors of the leaven in the lump, or the salt in the dish. We have already seen that one of the purposes of the Christian movement is to *be* a remnant, a prophetic community reflecting the life of God on earth; and at its best the Church has done this. It was the prophetic energy of Christians that overturned the slave trade, that campaigned for the civil rights of Black Americans, that helped to bring about the extraordinary revolutions we are witnessing in Eastern Europe, and that continues to care for the poor and destitute throughout the world. Mother Teresa in Calcutta is the most famous sign of this militant tendency in Christian history, but there are thousands of other examples, sung and unsung.

Nevertheless, in spite of these shining examples, our native inertia does conspire to keep us at home, nodding by our own fireside. The greatest triumph of evil is to persuade us that the universe is an absurdity and that moral action is quixotic. Some absurdists find an angry compassion within that gives them energy to live as though there were meaning in a meaningless universe; but some of them would echo Sartre: "Man is a useless passion. To get drunk by yourself in a bar, or to be a leader of the nations is equally pointless." The absurdist position, the conviction that the universe is without final meaning, is insidiously prevalent. As a philosophy it has produced its heroes and saints, but its general effect is to erode belief in a larger moral purpose and to fortify the type of private selfishness that seeks its own place in the sun for as long as it will shine.

The Christian answer, or the Christian way of living with the unanswerable question of evil and suffering, is to see it as a conflict between opposing principles that are battling to own us. Our own tiny and domestic struggles with indiscipline are parables of this larger universal struggle. It is still a conflict between the short-term pleasure of the instant good and the eternal pleasure for which we are destined. It is, indeed, happiness and delight that we crave, but our appetites and ambitions are too limited and we settle for the mere shadows of the grand delights our nature was made for. This is why temptation really feels like a battle. The acute discomfort of temptation, the obsessive needs that claw at us, are all signs that life is serious and the issues that confront us are momentous. Much of the answer we need, and most of the help in the struggle, comes from the meaning and work of Christ, whose death is a sign of the consequence of human evil, running without restraint. The crucifixion is a cartoon of the face of evil at its most grim. And yet, as we have attempted to show in this book, it is also a sign to us of the infinite and costly patience of God, who refuses to abandon us. It is the cross itself that gives us the strategy for our own liberation.

And this bring us back to George's broken body lying on the shingle at Brighton beach. We lost George from this life, were not able to save him, but his tragedy taught us many important things. First of all, there can be no healing without repentance. Repentance means that owning of our own condition, which is the essential prelude to renewal and growth. Sometimes the call to repentance appears to be stark and brutal. Those who have worked with alcoholics know all about the tough love that confronts the loved one with unpleasant truth. But the motive is salvation not flagellation. The toughness of the prophetic call is meant to penetrate the armour of our self-delusion and say, as Nathan the prophet said to David after his adultery with Bathsheba and the murder of her husband, "Thou art the man." This is the first inescapably painful step. We must own and confess our own weakness and need.

But fast upon this radical repentance, indeed, co-active with it, comes the gift of acceptance and forgiveness. We must know that we are understood and accepted, even while we are in this misery of our own making. We may have done evil but we must never be consigned to evil, otherwise we shall lose all hope, and hope is the energy that undermines the sovereignty of evil.

> Betwixt the stirrup and the ground
> Mercy I sought, mercy I found.[4]

We see both of these elements in the crucifixion, which stabs us to the heart with the knowledge of our own complicity in evil; and yet, at the same time, is a sign to us of the infinite pity and patience of God. The crucifixion is a cruel sacrament of God's love.

The final element in the process of sanctification is our constant dependence upon that energy of goodness we have called grace or Holy Spirit. It is never enough to *avoid* evil; we must enlist on the side of good and draw its energy into our own lives. And, as with everything else in the spiritual life, the efficacy of this approach can never be demonstrated theoretically in advance. It is known in the doing. We must perform the action if we would discover the meaning.

The three stages of repentance, acceptance and dependence – repentance of our sin, co-active with our acceptance by God, leading to a dynamic dependence upon the grace that is active in creation – have proved to be powerfully effective as Christians have struggled to live wisely. The three steps provide us with a pattern for the Christian life and its struggle with evil and sorrow. Christ gives us no philosophical answer to the problem of evil. Instead, he calls us to repent of our own evil, to accept forgiveness for it, and to co-operate with the grace of God in its battles against evil and its work of perfecting our own nature into the pattern of Christian holiness.

The Christian life was called a Way before it was called anything else – a way of life. It is a way of life that recognizes our weakness and constant need for forgiveness and acceptance. That continues to be part of its great appeal: in our guilt and wretchedness we need to know that we are loved with an eternal love. But the Christian way is more than a message of solace and comfort; it is also a way of power, the power of grace, the power of God's presence in our lives, enabling us to grow in strength and love.

Christ came to make us free and to help us live – and live more abundantly.

POSTSCRIPT

St Augustine ended his book on the Trinity with a long prayer to God in which he more or less apologized for the inadequacy of what he had written. He quoted the Book of Proverbs: "In much speaking thou shalt not escape sin", and meditated on the predicament of the person who uses words to try to escape the mystery of God. It is a most painful predicament, because the only alternative is silence and sometimes we have to speak; so the speaker or the writer who wrestles with the meaning and mystery of God is always defeated. I have often come away from a lecture or sermon I have delivered feeling unclean, somehow soiled by my own words. That feeling is even more pronounced at the end of a book that tries to explore the meaning of the Christian Gospel for today. Words cannot do it, but we have to go on spinning words, because we know that, as well as hiding God, they sometimes disclose God. But sometimes it is useful to try to distil many words into few.

Leslie Weatherhead once said that Gospel or good news is something that can be shouted across a street: "The war is over"; "The baby's born"; "Susan's out of danger". A good test of a spiritual message is just such a summary. How would I summarize the message of this book? In three short sentences that can be shouted across a street:

> God is for us.
> God forgives us.
> God helps us.

169

God is *for* us. In many religions and in many versions of the Christian religion this does not seem to be the case. They paint a picture of a cruel and arbitrary God who is against people, who is enraged by the mess they make, the muddles they get into, and wants to send most of them to hell. I've tried to explore some of the reasons why that picture of God emerged, but I am more intent on allowing the face of the God of mercy to show through the layers of grime that have obscured it. As the Letter of James puts it: "Mercy triumphs over judgement". So God is *for* us.

But we are not always for God. We create gaps between ourselves and God, partly out of the wrong sort of fear of God and partly our of sheer ignorance and confusion. But God in Christ forgives us and the gap we cannot bridge he reaches over. He meets us with his mercy. So God *forgives* us.

And God *helps* us. We are not on our own in time. There is an energy of goodness at work that we call grace or Holy Spirit. We can either co-operate with it or work against it. That energy of grace works in institutions and movements as well as in the individual soul, for the building of the kingdom of heaven on earth. That kingdom, that other country, is never fully established in time, but it is never completely effaced either and it continues to haunt our imagination, filling us with a holy discontent that sends us out to search for God's goodness, on earth as it is in heaven.

> God is for us.
> God forgives us.
> God helps us.

NOTES

1 ANOTHER COUNTRY

1 Stephen W. Hawking, *A Brief History of Time: From the Big Bang to black holes*, Bantam, 1988.
2 Sacheverell Sitwell, "Agamemnon's Tomb", *Selected Poems*, Duckworth 1948.
3 T.S. Eliot, "Little Gidding", *Collected Works*, Faber & Faber.
4 Maggie Ross, *Pillar of Flame: power, priesthood and spirituality*, SCM, 1988.
5 Thomas Carlyle, "Essay on Boswell's *Life of Johnson*".

2 ANOTHER KING

1 Augustine, *Confessions*, bk. 1, ch. I.
2 T.S. Eliot, "Little Gidding".

3 REJECTION

1 Laurence Binyon, "Prayers for the Fallen".
2 T.S. Eliot, "East Coker", *Collected Works*, Faber & Faber.
3 Austin Farrer, *Said or Sung*, Faith Press 1960, p.58.

4 RESTORATION

1 Austin Farrer, *Said or Sung*.
2 Ibid.
3 Matthew Arnold, "On Dover Beach"
4 John Betjeman, "A Lincolnshire Church".

5 SPIRIT

1 Gerard Manley Hopkins, "God's Grandeur".

6   CHURCH

1 Thomas Aquinas.

7   JUDGEMENT

1 James Joyce, *Portrait of the Artist as a Young Man*, Penguin, p.121.
2 Albert Schweitzer, *The Quest of the Historical Jesus*, SCM 1981, p.368.
3 Song from *West Side Story*, lyrics by Stephen Sondheim.
4 Alistair Cooke, *The Patient Has the Floor*, Bodley Head 1986, p.93.

8   MEANWHILE'

1 W.B. Yeats, "The Second Coming".
2 William Shakespeare, Sonnet CXXIX.
3 Yeats, "The Second Coming".
4 William Camden, "Remains. Epitaph for a Man Killed by Falling from His Horse".